C0-ARS-448

THE SOCIAL WORK MYSTIQUE

Toward a Sociology of Social Work

Marie A. Mathews

UNIVERSITY
PRESS OF
AMERICA

Copyright © 1981 by

University Press of America, Inc.

P.O. Box 19101, Washington, D.C. 20036

All rights reserved

Printed in the United States of America

ISBN (Perfect): 0-8191-1904-0
ISBN   (Cloth): 0-8191-1903-2

Library of Congress Catalog Card Number: **81-40723**

826195

LIBRARY
ALMA COLLEGE
ALMA, MICHIGAN

This book is dedicated to those social workers who have survived the Mystique of their profession, and especially to students, who come upon the Mystique with some disbelief, and who often prove to be wiser than their teachers.

ACKNOWLEDGMENTS

I am grateful to my mother and a variety of teachers who encouraged questions and a belief in the possibility of finding answers. More immediately, I thank my husband, a professor of philosophy, for being a patient listener and at times an impatient critic. Two friends and fellow faculty members have brought me viewpoints on the social work scene other than American: Dorothy Sarmiento (Oxford and Manchester), who introduced me to the work of Lady Barbara Wootton and shared drily incisive observations of the helping profession; and the late Katharine Radke (Tübingen), who maintained an abiding faith in the eventuality of social justice. I am deeply indebted for their help and encouragement.

Appreciation is extended to all of the publishers who have granted permission to quote from works cited, particularly the following:

To George Allen & Unwin Ltd., for permission to quote from Barbara Wootton, *Social Sciences and Social Pathology*, © 1959; and Eileen Younghusband, *Social Work and Social Change*, © 1964.

To Beacon Press and George Allen & Unwin Ltd., for permission to quote from Richard M. Titmuss, *Essays on the Welfare State*, © 1958.

To University of Toronto Press and George Allen & Unwin Ltd., for permission to quote from Barbara Wootton, *In a World I Never Made: Autobiographical Reflections*, © 1967.

To University of Toronto Press and Routledge & Kegan Paul Ltd., for permission to quote from Kathleen Woodroofe, *From Charity to Social Work in England and the United States*, © 1962, 1964.

To Oxford University Press, for permission to quote from T.S. Simey and M.B. Simey, *Charles Booth, Social Scientist*, © 1960.

To Faber and Faber Ltd., for permission to quote from *Social Case-Work in Great Britain*, edited by Cherry Morris, 2nd Edition, © 1955.

To Loyola University Press, for permission to quote from Felix F. Biestek, *The Casework Relationship*, © 1957.

To *The American Sociologist*, for permission to quote from Vol. 8, no. 4 (November 1973).

To *The Social Service Review*, for permission to quote from Vol. 41, no. 4 (December 1967).

To Macmillan Publishing Co., Inc., for permission to quote from *Mass Society in Crisis*, edited by Rosenberg, Gerven, and Howton, © 1964.

To Harcourt Brace Jovanovich, Inc., for permission to quote from Bernard Berelson and Gary A. Steiner, *Human Behavior: An Inventory of Scientific Findings*, © 1964.

To Prentice-Hall, Inc., Englewood Cliffs, N.J., for permission to quote from William Schofield, *Psychotherapy: The Purchase of Friendship*, © 1964.

To Russell Sage Foundation, for permission to quote from Mary Richmond, *The Long View*, © 1930.

To the National Council on Crime and Delinquency, for permission to quote from *Crime and Delinquency*, Vol. XIV, no. 1 (January 1968).

To Jossey-Bass Inc., Publishers, for permission to quote from Philip Klein, *From Philanthropy to Social Welfare*, © 1968.

To Random House, Inc., for permission to quote from Florence Hollis, *Casework: A Psychosocial Therapy*, © 1964.

To Family Service Association of America, for permission to quote from *Social Casework*, Vol. XLII, no. 8 (October 1961).

To John M. Martin and Joseph P. Fitzpatrick, for permission to quote from *Delinquent Behavior: A Redefinition of the Problem*, © 1964.

To Harper & Row, Publishers, Inc., for permission to quote from Robert E. L. Faris, *Chicago Sociology, 1920–1932*, © 1967, 1970.

To The University of Chicago Press, for permission to quote from *Social Service Review*, Vol. XXVII, no. 1 (March 1953); Vol. XXIX, no. 1 (March 1955); Vol. XXXI, no. 1 (March 1957); Vol. XLI, no. 4 (December 1967); Introduction to Robert E. L. Faris, *Chicago Sociology, 1920–1932*, © 1967, 1970; Philip Abrams, *The Origins of British Sociology*, 1834–1914, © 1968.

To Columbia University Press, New York, for permission to quote from *Social Work Practice 1965*, © 1965; *Issues in American Social Work*, edited by A. J. Kahn, © 1959; and R. E. Smalley, *Theory for Social Work Practice*, © 1967.

To Council on Social Work Education for permission to quote from *Journal of Education for Social Work*, Vol. I, no. 1 (Spring

1965); Vol. I, no. 2 (Fall 1965); Vol. II, no. 1 (Spring 1966); Vol. IV, no. 2 (Fall 1968); Vol. VI, no. 1 (Spring 1970); Vol. VI, no. 2 (Fall 1970); Vol. VII, no. 2 (Spring 1971); Vol. X, no. 2 (Spring 1974); Vol. XIII, no. 1 (Winter 1977); Vol. XIII, no. 2 (Spring 1977): and *Official Statement of Curriculum Policy for the Master's Degree Program in Graduate Professional Schools of Social Work*, 1962.

To the National Association of Social Workers, Inc., for permission to quote from *Social Work*, Vol. 1, no. 1 (January 1956), © 1956; Vol. 2, no. 3 (July 1957), © 1957; Vol. 7, no. 2 (April 1962), © 1962; Vol. 8, no. 3 (July 1963), © 1963; *Encyclopedia of Social Work*, 16th Edition, Vol. 2, © 1971; and *Centrally Planned Change: Prospects and Concepts*, edited by Robert Morris, © 1964.

INTRODUCTION

The 1960s, decade of civil and student revolt, included a generally unheralded anniversary. The year 1969 marked the 100th anniversary of modern social work, the most institutionalized of society's academic helping routes. The centennial of the founding of the Charity Organisation Society of England passed largely unnoticed in America, as did Dame Eileen Younghusband's earlier (1964) invitation to interested parties to journey through social work's past to assess its successes and failures.

There was no mention of the founding event in the *Journal of Education for Social Work*, official organ of the Council on Social Work Education, launched in 1965 to herald social work's "coming of age as a profession."

This neglect by social work educators representing the major accrediting agency is understandable enough, if one comprehends the reluctance of the profession to associate itself with the often crotchety and unlovable charity methodologists who comprised the C.O.S.

Lack of interest on the part of the public is even more understandable. The proliferation of helping movements, especially since the 1960s, involving several academic disciplines, as well as community groups of paraprofessionals and nonprofessionals, has created new groups of social workers not particularly concerned with formal distinctions in helping roles.

Nevertheless, the direction taken by the Charity Organisation Society, as modern social work's beginning and first historical option, is not without theoretical and practical consequences both for social work and the general public: for social work, because the profession currently is suffering severe dilemmas on all levels of performance, as the *Journal of Education for Social Work* reveals, despite its promise of maturity for the profession; for the general public, because of the deep concern over the wide diversity of viewpoints on the success of helping efforts.

The Charity Organisation Society seems, at first, an unlikely place to find firm theoretical and practical footing for a fresh perspective on social problems far removed from the Victorian Age. It is only fair to note that my own interest was accidental. As a sociologist teaching at and participating for a year in a curricular revision of a school of social service, I found myself confronted with a series of nagging questions about the relationship between the theoretical and practical, combined with a long-held optimistic feeling that we must know better than we do. The confusion involved in the process of deciding what social workers do, to whom, and on what socially sanctioned grounds was enormous.

I had not yet read Dame Younghusband's invitation to assess social work's history when I began my informal odyssey through the voluminous and contradictory literature of options, problems, resolutions, and present official positions. Nor was I yet convinced of Younghusband's caveat that the journey would show that "there is nothing to be complacent about" (1964, p. 15).

Previous contacts with social workers were sporadic and, admittedly, not positive enough to make me want to become a part of the team: some beginning courses and field work before a change of majors at the Master's level; interaction during some seven years' work with delinquents, in court and institutional settings; the earliest contact, while employed at Chicago's Back of the Yards Neighborhood Council.

To be unconvinced, however, is not necessarily to be hostile. I had remained impressed with social work dedication and sanguine about the inevitability of some rapprochement between the art and social science theories. My ultimate disappointment in the lack of progress was to be all the greater because of my initial hopefulness.

The level of discussion during the curricular study, the quality of textbooks, and the intensity of student complaints and faculty discontent suggested, in fact, that we may very well be doing better than we know.

The curricular involvement raised another concern. The rigidity with which the professionals pursued traditional, action-oriented methods and values, and the corresponding lack of rigor with which they pursued a scientific framework and its methodology, seemed strangely alien to the free spirit and vocabulary of inquiry commonly associated with the academic area. The indoctrination of students, faculty, and clients not only lacked the graceful fluidity of an art form but carried a harsh aura of censure for discussion, even in areas where official literature lamented the profession's failure.

The analogue came much later: Topsy, social work's name for its offspring, had not grown up, scientifically and professionally. She was alternately child and imperious queen, insisting on a shifting orthodoxy. Dissidents were treated with head-chopping.

A significant rapprochement had not taken place between social work and the scientific lending disciplines. Despite heroic adherence to the value of the work ethic on the part of social work educators, no happy alliance seemed at hand unless a new direction were to be taken without equivocation.

The questions became imperative: Why the deadening defensiveness? What had happened in social work's past to produce this unhappy state of the present?

There is no definitive history of social work, and what follows is not intended as such. A search through social work's history reveals several distinct options taken by the profession. Serious limitations of these historical choices eventually needed explanation and modern reworking. Precisely because the choices were not recognized clearly as selected solutions among other possibilities, the end result, the socializing framework, became *a social work mystique.*

It is this social work mystique that adds a new share of confusion to perennial problems of alignment between the theoretical and the practical, the individual and the social. This mystique has allowed social workers to assert a unique type of social work knowledge, a special methodology, and perennial confidence in the inevitability of progress, despite failures and not clearly remedied mistakes.

At the time of its 100th anniversary, social work faced another historical option: a mature alignment with the concerns and concepts of the broader academic community, particularly the social sciences. As a sociologist, it is inevitable that I should be concerned primarily with social work's relationship to sociology and with the direction of my own interest, the beginnings of a sociology of social work.

Social work desperately needs sociology, as it needs the other social sciences and the best of the methodology and language of the academic community. I should not like to be accused, however, of seeing sociology as social work's savior, both because I have been warned against such a position by social work colleagues and, more properly, because I am quite aware that sociology has problems of its own.

In the applied area, Donald Tarter (1973) urges sociologists to heed Skinner's call for the development of a social technology and concludes that, at present, "sociology is a science without a technology." Further, he prophesizes: "Technology has traditionally served as the action arm of science, testing theoretical concepts and opening new vistas of application. A science without technology is doomed to the monotony of repetitive observation and idle speculation" (p. 153). In 1965, Gouldner and Miller presented a case for the existence of beginning applied sociology (p. vii).

Tracing the relationship between social work and sociology— and, peripherally, exploring some other possible options—will provide only a part of the answer to the modern problems of the helping professions. The Charity Organisation Society, which began the modern process we call professional social work, seized upon a limited method as total solution to the 19th century problems of urbanization and industrialization.

If we see ourselves as confused, the C.O.S. originators did not, and it is refreshing to make their acquaintance. If we conclude that their approach was shortsighted, there is ample evidence that we have not come to grips with the questions their approach raised.

CONTENTS

A CENTURY OF SERVICE: 1869–1969

In 1969, professional social work marked the centennial of its origins in the old Charity Organisation Society of England, founded 100 years earlier. Though some prefer to see the beginning of social work in the establishment of professional societies or requisites for graduate training, and others, in the Judeo-Christian tradition, there is ample evidence for regarding the founding of the C.O.S. as the start of the modern social work movement. The founding members of the Charity Organisation Society have been called both "grandparents" (Younghusband, 1964, p. 15) and "beginnings" (Woodroofe, 1962, p. 24) of the social work profession, as well as "pioneers" (Wootton, 1959, p. 268) of modern social casework, the oldest and most developed of the profession's methods.

The comment of one long-time public welfare client, surveying the latest fledgling case worker, is not inappropriate to the observance of the profession's century of service: "I certainly have trained a lot of social workers."

If 100 years of service suggest a staggering number of clients, that amorphous human group whose needs and problems stubbornly exceed professional social work's capacity to meet them, nonetheless, as disciplines go, social work is still in its youth.

The beginnings of professional social work make it only a slightly younger half-sibling of the science, or (depending on one's persuasion) the discipline, of sociology. In terms of achievement, however, social work and sociology may be considered at different respective stages in their rites of passage toward full professional and scientific adulthood. Younghusband (1964) sees professional social work as still in its infancy, although, she claims, it has taken several centuries to bring it to birth. Among "its more remote ancestors" she includes Vives, St. Vincent de Paul, Count Rumford, and Thomas Chalmers. The "grandparents of social work in this country are typified by the Charity Organisation Society and the police court missioners" (p. 15).

When the members of the Society for Organising Charitable Relief and Repressing Mendicity met for the first time in Willis's Rooms in March, 1870, they laid the foundation on which, "more than any other, . . . social casework was evolved," "very much the product of nineteenth century individualism" (Woodroofe, 1962, pp. 24, 54). Thus began the first and most highly developed of the three methods of social work.

Despite social work's youth, however, there has been no definitive historical work, starting with the C.O.S. and charting the theoretical and practical problems and adaptations of the profession in an orderly and analytic progression (Beck, 1959, p. 193).

Training for Social Work: Third International Survey (United Nations, 1958) admits to knowing of no comparative study of the discoveries and methods of such social pioneers as Vives, St. Vincent de Paul, Count Rumford, Thomas Chalmers, Canon Barnett, Octavia Hill, and Jane Addams in the West and Gokhale, Gandhi, and others in the East in relation to modern discoveries about the processes of work in community development (p. 74).

There is no general theory book that a teacher might put into the hands of a beginning student or, for that matter, into the hands of an interested observor who shared the view of Richard Titmuss (1958): "The social services (however we define them) can no longer be considered as 'things apart'; as phenomena of marginal interest, like looking out of the window on a train journey. They are a part of the journey itself. They are an integral part of industrialization" (Preface).

What is happening to social work is of obvious interest not only to teachers channeling youthful concern into socially realistic pathways, or to students choosing to make a lifetime investment in the helping services; what is happening to social work is, or should be, of interest to the general public, who, in various ways, help to support the institution of professional social work as a formal caretaker for society's concern for its own social environment.

In 1964, Dame Eileen Younghusband, British doyenne of social work, offered a brief but convincing rationale for public concern: "No society can afford to employ people to be more or less harmless nor can we risk their doing harm" (p. 29).

It is difficult to assess present or past social work effectiveness. Social workers are understandably defensive about such critiques as Marion K. Sander's "Social Work: A Profession Chasing Its Tail" (1957) or the genuinely funny and often perceptive movie *A Thousand Clowns* (1965).

What there is to know about social work may be found in a voluminous literature—journal articles, texts, theoretical and historical statements—as well as in the classroom, in the field, from professional organizations, and lastly, and, perhaps, most interestingly, from the private conversations of social workers themselves.

The techniques of oral history, applied to practicing social workers, might prove to be the best means of capturing the current spirit and present dilemmas of the over-100-year-old discipline.

With some exceptions, such as Philip Klein or Lady Barbara Wootton, critics usually are content with a punchy foray into the field. I first discovered Lady Barbara Wootton's relatively short essay on "Contemporary Attitudes in Social Work" (1959) through the help of a British friend, as dismayed as I was with the inadequacy of certain positions. I still consider Wootton's criticism the most trenchant, though social workers like to believe her comments are "old hat," and rumor has it that her criticism was kept from graduate students in some schools.

Philip Klein's *From Philanthropy to Social Welfare* (1968) of necessity discusses social work in his excellent survey of social welfare in the United States, but Klein shows some resistance to sociological alliance as a valid part of the solution.

Social Work: The Unloved Profession (1973), by Willard Richan and Allan R. Mendelsohn, identifies social work's therapeutic mission as the key to the abandonment of its historic commitment to human welfare and the poor in favor of a new focus on the suburbanite. Mendelsohn sees a future alliance between social workers and the academic world as doomed; Richan hopes for university and professional reform. Both authors argue for elimination of schools of social work in the traditional sense.

There have been critiques of various aspects of the social work process, such as Paul Halmos's *The Faith of the Counsellors* (1966), which examines the deficiencies of social work's Freudian emphasis.

Updated works by social workers for social workers, such as Ruth Smalley's *Theory for Social Work Practice* (1967) and Florence Hollis's *Casework: A Psychosocial Therapy* (1964), are essentially ameliorative and professionally optimistic.

In addition, the present mood of students is ahistorical: they usually are eager to get on with the job of helping people, solving problems as they arise.

As for social scientists, they generally have enough trouble making their own historical beginnings and theoretical problems palatable to the eager mind. In earlier days, sociology teachers looked with some favor on students who came to sociology with a background in social work, or who, taking the opposite route, went into social work after some background in sociology.

That view has changed. There is less encouragement for professionals in other disciplines to ferret out connecting links with social work. Peter Berger (1963), for example, neatly severs the perceived tie between sociology and social work by asserting that social work "doctrine" has not only very little to do with sociology, "but it is marked, indeed, by a singular obtuseness with regard to social reality" (p. 4).

3

What reason do we have, then, for a journey into social work literature, a journey more closely resembling that of Alice in Wonderland than professional social workers would like to admit? In this case, it is a journey into Social-Land with Topsy, social work's affectionate name for its sometimes misguided and unpredictable progeny.

What impulse propels us to race through 100 years of aims, resolutions, techniques, and "philosophy," only to find to our bewilderment at the end that the movement scarcely has budged an inch? "But of course," as the Queen explained to Alice, "you have to run fast to stay where you are."

In 1964, Younghusband invited professional colleagues and others to pause and review the development of social work "in order to try to understand what we discovered, what we have achieved, what we have lost by the way, and what objectives we should try to set ourselves for the future" (p. 15).

It is not for the faint-hearted to accept Younghusband's invitation. Younghusband herself predicts that the excursion will not induce complacency, "for there is nothing to be complacent about" (p. 15).

First, the literature of the field is not only voluminous and scattered, but disturbingly contradictory and disconnected.

Second, dialogue with critics in and out of the profession too often is handled in a manner reminiscent of the techniques used to subdue and confuse Alice on the Queen's croquet ground.

Alice, it will be remembered, was sure she had not as yet any dispute with the Queen, but felt it might happen any moment. She had reason to be apprehensive, knowing the general fondness for beheading people in Wonderland. "I don't think they play at all fairly," she complained, "and they all quarrel so dreadfully one can't hear oneself speak—and they don't seem to have any rules in particular; at least, if there are, nobody attends to them."

Social work's rules for dialogue about her helping past and present are a shifting mixture, allowing, in turn, for uncoordinated spurts of agonizing self-recrimination, happy hopefulness in the net effect of dedicated if ineffective results, and defensively belligerent gamesmanship against academic analysis.

Third, there is a feeling among social workers—a common human reaction in exaggerated form—that any criticism of an intellectual position is a criticism of social workers themselves, many of whom are dedicated, long suffering, and misused, and a good many of whom are emancipated from the theoretical limitations of official professional postures. Many are personal friends.

Fourth, equally threatening to analysis is the assumption that, to make comments about social work, one must at the same time thoroughly assess all the inadequacies in the social sciences from which social work might derive a new theoretical base.

4

There really is no need to be defensive. No integrated science of human behavior exists, much less an integrated frame of reference for application.

Berelson and Steiner, in *Human Behavior: An Inventory of Scientific Findings* (1964), note the conclusions of "distinguished scholars in the major disciplines of the behavioral sciences" (p. 4).

Speaking for anthropology, Clyde Kluckhohn concluded in 1957: " 'Anthropologists of all branches have been so preoccupied with field work that the profession has not organized and assimilated what is in fact "known" ' " (Berelson and Steiner, 1964, p. 4).

Ernest Hilgard said of psychology in 1957: " 'The state of factual knowledge is not very satisfactory: neither is it very easy to remedy. The number of dependable "facts" in the various fields of psychology are not very impressive' " (p. 4).

Of sociology, Edward Shils noted in 1948: " 'Nothing is more necessary at present than the systematic coalition and "shaking down" of American sociological research results to discover what they amount to, to weigh the evidence on crucial problems and to see what is really known on the basis of adequate evidence and what is still unsettled' " (p. 4).

Finally, before we begin a journey into social work's past, it must be admitted that the largest part of the story already is known. Alfred Kadushin, as professor of the School of Social Work at the University of Wisconsin, concluded in 1965 that social work is not graduate work, either in nature or level of content (pp. 33–46).

Dr. William H. Form (1964), in a workshop conducted in 1963, summed up the effect of the socialization workers receive from their literature and schools. Social work as a profession, he said, "tends to breed a type that is timid, conservative, unimaginative, and easily co-opted by the tough-minded" (p. 89).

In short, what seems abundantly clear is that the profession of social work today faces many serious theoretical and practical dilemmas in every area. What is not equally clear from a reading of the current literature is that the profession is prepared to handle its present problems—some would say "crisis"—with a clear eye to those historical options that have produced the theoretical and practical consequences observed today.

The literature of professional social work does not assure the reader that the profession will meet its current dilemmas without resorting to the problem-solving defense of its *mystique*.

This is sufficient reason for a journey back to social work's origins with the founders of the old Charity Organisation Society. If Topsy subsequently grew without plan, she is not social work's child alone. She started out as a possible, if mistaken, option in the minds of a group of people consumed with the notion of a methodical philanthropy. As such, she is part and parcel of the historical legacy of social problem solving.

5

As Younghusband asserts, "No society can afford to employ people to be more or less harmless nor can we risk their doing harm."

In America, as events unfolded, social work leadership concluded in the 70's that what they had perceived as a "coming of age" in 1965 turned out in reality to be a major crisis in all areas—a serious misjudgment by professionals.

In Britain by 1979, after some 3,000 social workers ended a six-month strike, the recipients of social work's aid—the general public—took it upon themselves to reach their own conclusions, aired in British newspapers and media. Grievances ranged from useless, incompetent, to sometimes harmful social work ministrations.

The following journey into social work's past does not constitute a definitive history. It is an acceptance of the invitation to see what is to be found in a journey through social work's literature—looking at social work through social workers' eyes.

That journey reveals definite historical options, which social work explains ambiguously. Consequences of the options and explanations lead me to conclusions somewhat different from those of other critics.

THE C.O.S.: THE FIRST OPTION

If the origins of the Charity Organisation Society are obscure, and controversy rages about its founders, "the conditions which provoked the Society into existence in 1869 are beyond dispute" (Woodroofe, 1962, p. 25). The conditions which prompted a new group of method humanitarians to seek principles for the ordering of charity (side by side with the Poor Law and a disorderly philanthropy) were, very simply, the manifestations of poverty in the midst of Victorian plenty.

"The C.O.S. of course discovered just what its name said—the importance of organizing charity."

> This meant instead of indiscriminate doles a thorough investigation of each case, making a plan in cooperation with the applicant, always giving adequate help if you helped at all, seeing a case through to the end once you had taken it on, only helping the deserving, and keeping full records of what you had done. (Younghusband, 1964, p. 15)

It is these organizers of charity that Younghusband titles the "grandparents of social work in this country," in conjunction with the police court missioners, who, some seven years after the founding of the C.O.S., came into existence to offer a personal relationship rather than material help.

The Charity Organisation Society, at times described as founded by Edward Denison and Octavia Hill, carried on the rationalization of benevolence or the organization of "scientific" philanthropy, both in England and in the United States. With few exceptions, says Klein (1968), American schools of social work training have remained within the sphere of influence of the charity organization movement (p. 224).

The matters with which modern social work deals are old, says Woodroofe (1962), but the "beginnings" of the profession are to be found in the Charity Organisation Society of the 1860s, which offered "one" answer to the problem of poverty amidst Victorian plenty (p. 3).

In Younghusband's view, modern casework "so far as its principles are concerned, is rooted in the Judaeo-Christian and democratic traditions of respect for the value of each individual person" (1964, p. 17). Social workers "have a respectable ancestry in religion, science, and the great reform movements" (p. 26).

Younghusband further merges the profession with such disparate ancestors as St. Vincent de Paul (p. 25) and, by implication, having claimed a linkage with the great reform movements, the economists of the 19th century, Charles Booth, and the socialist Webbs (p. 37), even though she clearly sees the C.O.S. and the reformers as having chosen separate paths. Speaking of the mutual dislike of the Fabian socialists and the C.O.S., Younghusband concludes: "In the end both were right and both were wrong" (p. 16). "The environmentalists and those who emphasized personal service, the forerunners of social caseworkers, were both right" (p. 26).

The historical fact is that Woodroofe, the Senior Lecturer in History, relates social work's beginnings more accurately than does Younghusband, the social worker. The C.O.S. was only *one* of the responses made in Victorian England to the problems of poverty. That response in no way encompassed the potential of the Judeo-Christian tradition to inform religious, scientific, or humanistic viewpoints.

This question of origins and value systems is the first area in which the voyager into social work's past will notice considerable inconsistency. An account of the availability of fascinating alternative routes to the one chosen by the C.O.S. would make a colorful beginning for the first year social work student seeking to understand the relationship of poverty to the problems of the modern world.

If casework principles are rooted in the Judeo-Christian and democratic traditions, the initial thrust of the C.O.S. was far more secular, human-centered, and pragmatic than some of the doctrinal creeds of that day or this. It is precisely because social work was initiated in the spirit of a secular religion of humanity that its own problem of religion as value was later to surface as a difficulty.

Certainly, the spirit of the C.O.S. was not the spirit of St. Vincent de Paul, even if the Sisters of Charity organized by St. Vincent also investigated cases and were careful to distinguish the fully or partially self-supporting poor, as Woodroofe alleges (1962, p. 44). Beatrice Webb observed in 1926 that almsgiving, to the unsophisticated Christian, "even of the nineteenth century," was essentially a religious exercise, a manifestation of one's love of God. "Charity was, to the orthodox Christian, not a process by which a given end could be attained, but an end in itself" (p. 191). *Monsieur Vincent's* Sisters were exemplars of a pristine dedication.

How opposite, noted Webb, was the state of mind and conduct of the new mid-Victorian philanthropists. "To the pioneer of the new philanthropy, 'to give unto every one who asketh thee' was a mean and cruel form of self-indulgence" (p. 192).

Webb quotes from that "great Scot," Robert [sic] Chalmers, pioneer of charity reform in the first half of the 19th century—a pioneer whom Younghusband also includes in the life blood of modern social work. Chalmers's position stands in contrast to that of Clement of Alexandria, who warned the faithful not to judge who is deserving and who undeserving: " 'For by being fastidious and setting thyself to try who are fit for thy benevolence, and who are not, it is possible that thou mayest neglect some who are friends of God' " (Webb, p. 192, n. 19).

Thus, in spite of some vogue among those who counted themselves enlightened, the C.O.S. "found small acceptance among the Christian Churches, any more than among the impulsive giver of alms" (p. 197).

Webb concludes that well-to-do men and women of good will, the pioneers of organized charity, unwittingly made an ominous discovery. "By rudely tearing off the wrappings of mediaeval almsgiving disguising the skeleton at the feast of capitalist civilization, they had let loose the tragic truth that wherever society is divided into a minority of 'Haves' and a multitude of 'Have Nots,' charity is twice cursed, it curseth him that gives and him that takes" (pp. 196–197).

If the C.O.S. did not represent charity in its purest form, neither did the society represent the most enlightened democratic view of the value of the individual, for the client's "right to make his own decisions about his life is a tenet to which the early social workers unfortunately did not subscribe" (Younghusband, 1964, p. 17).

Just as the social services in England, as late as the early 20th century, cannot be understood apart from the particular culture in which they grew up (Titmuss, 1958), so, too, was an earlier sociology colored by the valuations of the 19th century.

Loch, the Protagonist

Charles Stewart Loch, who became Secretary of the C.O.S. in 1875 and "piloted" the Society through the next 38 years as "chief vendor" of its principles (Woodroofe, 1962, p. 28), is an interesting protagonist of certain 19th-century values, and, hence, of beginning social work. Loch was looking to create "a Church of Charity." " 'If Charity is to fulfil her mission, she cannot suffer herself to be made either the servant or the nurse of even the most vigorous sectarianism' " (p. 31). Loch " 'made the C.O.S.; he was the C.O.S.' " (p. 29).

Had he been born 50 years earlier, Woodroofe concludes, Loch would have entered the Church, and, indeed, Loch apparently had toyed with the idea of Church service (p. 31). But because "his social

9

conscience had already been stirred into life, mainly by a sense of guilt born of 'some vague regret' that the lives of others, judged by his own, were 'sunless and sad' " (p. 30), Loch chose instead a life of social service.

With Loch's sense of guilt was combined "a desire for action, in which he could play a part to set the world right. . . . But more important than either a sense of guilt or a desire for action was Loch's strong instinct for service" (p. 30).

These motives, says Woodroofe, were well understood and shared by many of his contemporaries engaged in welfare work. The individual guilt complexes of many Lochs combined to produce what Beatrice Webb called a "class consciousness of sin," born of the increasing gap between rich and poor caused by a burgeoning industrialization (Woodroofe, 1962, p. 22; see Younghusband, 1964, p. 17). Webb herself, however, denied that the estimable leaders of the C.O.S., unlike many of their contemporaries, had the faintest glimmer of her "class consciousness of sin" (1926, pp. 199–200).

Armed, then, with the especial motivation of his day and the premise that the individual was to take provision for himself and his family lest both he and society be demoralized, Loch "preached and popularized" his thesis of charity with evangelical fervor.

> Often he was so defensive that even today his writings splutter with rage. The charge that C.O.S. was solely a relief organization, or that it was concerned mainly with a detection of fraud . . . or that people starved while inquiries were being made always put him in war-like mood, but in calmer moments, his exposition of his philosophy of Charity has both eloquence and grace. (Woodroofe, 1962, p. 32)

Despite his defensiveness, however, it was to Loch that Mary E. Richmond, American social worker *par excellence*, felt constrained to trace affiliation and indebtedness. " 'There is not a family social worker in America today, not a social case worker of any sort, in fact —who does not owe him a heavy debt' " (Woodroofe, 1962, p. 29).

The Society had two broad aims: (1) by the use of well-defined principles, to introduce order into the chaos of London's philanthropic organizations and to reduce the incidence of pauperism; and (2) "repressing mendicity." Only cases considered deserving of help were to be treated, thereby not only reducing needless expenditures, but using charity to increase the moral stature both of the individual and society. Indiscriminate charity demoralized and encouraged habits of thriftlessness and dependence.

The root causes of poverty and pauperism, in the collective mind of the C.O.S., were such habits as thriftlessness and dependence.

In short, a nonsectarian humanism, combined with a distaste for disorderly philanthropy and a desire to bring some principles to service, was a striking value of the 19th century. In this respect, the 19th century still reflected the emotional undertones of the 1601

Poor Law, which through many revisions had continued to distinguish between the deserving and the undeserving poor.

Loch himself expressed dislike for state old-age pensions and declared he would not barter his "Charity" for a dozen "Social Welfares" (Woodroofe, 1962, p. 30).

However, despite Loch's clear association with the beginnings of modern social work—despite the fact that his papers reveal theoretical foundations on which early concepts of social work were built (Woodroofe, 1962, p. 30)—the image of the fervent evangelist was destined to become unpalatable to the professional social worker.

Woodroofe speaks to Loch's passing from the list of respected ancestors: "Today, however, mainly owing to profound changes in social conditions and in ways of thought, many of Loch's ideas have been ignored or discredited. . . . some of his writings, too, breathe a class-consciousness galling to a generation more embarrassed about class-distinctions than his own; and even his favorite term 'Charity' . . . now has emotional connotations universally disliked" (pp. 29–30).

Denial of one's roots can be an impediment to healthy identity formation, and social workers admit they are undergoing a painful identity search today. Parenthetically, it should be noted that if the *Journal of Education for Social Work*, launched in the spring of 1965 to herald "Social Work's coming of age as a profession," did not advert to the 100th anniversary of its founding in the Charity Organisation Society, neither did it mention its zealous first secretary.

To the observer, members of the C.O.S. represent comfort and security amid the whiplash of forward and backward movements characteristic of social work's history. If one does not agree with the direction chosen by social work's founders, in view of other possible options, nevertheless their aims are clear and dedicated. More important, their aims are part of a broader direction taken by the Western world to solve the problem of modern poverty. The intellectual and emotional assessments of the poor embedded in the famous English Poor Law are, in essence, those of the C.O.S.

The English Poor Law

For modern purposes, the C.O.S. response of a methodized charity may be seen as a centuries-later reaction to a whole series of adaptations growing out of the statute of 1536, sometimes known as England's first poor law. This statute, though concentrating chiefly on the organization of voluntary funds for the relief of those unable to work, and lacking appropriate administrative machinery, represented a new approach to the problem of poverty.

The statute of 1536 prohibited begging and indiscriminate charity. It sought to classify the poor into those categories that ultimately were to be accepted by the C.O.S.: "deserving" and "undeserving." The aged and infirm were in need of relief; poor children were to be apprenticed.

Following a series of modifications, the Old Poor Law of 1601, made permanent in 1623, was to establish the tone, the basic assumptions, and the machinery for dealing with the poor well into the 20th century. By the terms of the Old Poor Law, the parish, Britain's smallest unit of government, became the administrative agent for a poor rate levied on all householders. The funds were to be used to relieve and provide for the miseries of the aged, if necessary with cottages on the wasteland or commons; poor children were to be apprenticed, and the able poor set to work.

It is not necessary to detail the legal and administrative changes which the Poor Law underwent: the literature on the subject is ample. Nor is it necessary to consider the benefits of organized relief over the unorganized relief of the era preceding the Poor Law.

What is important to note are some of the prevailing attitudes toward the poor represented by selected Poor Law modifications. The concept of eligibility of residence, to ensure against an influx of indigents to overburdened parishes, for example, was established in the Law of Settlement and Removal of 1662. The indigent, in some cases, could obtain residence by serving an apprenticeship within the parish or working as a servant for one year. In some rural parishes, efforts were made to remove families overburdened with children.

Perhaps the segment of the population best served by the Poor Law were the bona fide resident aged and sick, though, by 1693, none of these was to be given aid except in emergency and with the authority of a justice, and eligibility for the small monthly allowances was to be reviewed annually.

By the act of 1697, the quaint requirement that paupers distinguish themselves by wearing a large red or blue P on their outer garments went into effect.

The Speenhamland System of 1795 was a departure in a decidedly modern vein. The justices of Berkshire, in the district of Speenhamland, decided that wages below an absolute minimum should be supplemented by the parish in accordance with the price of bread and the number of dependents.

The Speenhamland System's merits are debated to this day (see Matza, 1971). Thomas Chalmers, whom Younghusband lists as one of social work's ancestors, concluded that "no evil genius could have designed a system of greater malignity for the corruption of the race" ("Poor Law," 1966, p. 224). David Matza (1971) credits Speenhamland, along with the harsh Poor Law reform of 1834, with "a major replenishing" of disreputable poverty (p. 645).

Matza himself adopts an intermediate position. He believes that the category of disreputable poverty is a product of prejudice, without substantial foundation, but that the poor are readily susceptible to the immobilization and demoralization implicit in the concept of disreputable poverty. He notes that the massive generation of pauperism does occur occasionally under special conditions (pp. 644–645). His own solution is admittedly nonspecific in terms of process, but he places his faith in a humane democratic socialism (p. 656).

The point to be made is that, by summarily dismissing their ancestors, social workers dismiss part of legitimate welfare history, some of which is reflected in attitudes that prevail today. There is no question that one's estimation of the wisdom of Speenhamland rests ultimately on social philosophical assumptions about the nature of man in society and the obligations in justice of the community toward its less fortunate members. If Loch's beloved word "Charity" has fallen into some disrepute, it is partly because of a better understanding of the nature of justice.

At any rate, the New Poor Law of 1834 reinforced more clearly a notion of the poor that was evident from the beginning. The Commissioners of 1834 stated it thus: "Every penny bestowed that tends to render the condition of the pauper more eligible than that of the independent laborer is a bounty on indolence and vice" ("Poor Law," 1966, p. 224).

Poverty, a crime, must be stigmatized to enforce the prevailing conclusion that not Providence but the poor themselves are the cause of their disrepute. Outdoor relief was abolished, and indigents were to be saved from their own sloth by being sent to the workhouse for relief.

The terrors of the workhouse, which indiscriminately lumped together the aged, the sick, children, and the able-bodied poor, may be surmised from reports that some laborers were willing to accept as little as five or six shillings a week rather than declare themselves paupers.

By 1871, a local government board assumed central authority. Relief recipients not only were subject to a special regimen, but were compelled to wear pauper garments. They also were shorn of their civil and political rights, including the right to vote. Disfranchisement of the pauper was not repealed until 1918, although criticism and amelioration of the worst conditions of the workhouse were made occasionally before that time.

Functionaries, Social Workers

Regardless of the merits of organizing charity in a growing industrial economy, the consequences of the Poor Law, besides abuses directed at the poor, included the emergence both of administrative

13

functionaries and social workers—two categories of personnel at times indistinguishable from each other.

In the C.O.S. phase, and indeed well into the 20th century, "the social worker's function was to distribute alms in such a way, and with such safeguards, as to encourage the virtues of thrift, self-help and independence, acting, it would seem, on what Mr. (now Lord) Attlee has called the 'general assumption that all applicants are frauds unless they prove themselves otherwise' " (Wootton, 1959, p. 268).

C.O.S. representatives, while deploring some of the excesses of the Poor Law before the reform commission of 1905, nevertheless were unwilling to depart from their fundamental view of the poor as needing supervision and counsel by an army of trained general or family caseworkers, and constant surveillance to ensure that the poor would not become public charges.

Based on this view, says Wootton, the founders of the Charity Organisation Society resolutely opposed the introduction of old-age pensions, school dinners, and similar measures, though occasionally they did raise their voices in support of the few social reforms which they felt to be compatible with the virtues to be inculcated into the lower classes (p. 258).

Characterization of these Charity Organisation Society founders depends, as in the assessment of the Poor Law, not only on the facts at hand, but on one's view of the world and the place of the poor in it.

Lady Barbara Wootton, who admits to an outspoken agnosticism and socialism, deplores the "inquisitorial methods" by which charitably disposed well-to-do persons sought protection for themselves and the community against the threats inherent in the payment of unearned income to the poor, "though not, apparently, to the rich" (1959, p. 271).

Eileen Younghusband, on the other hand, a famous representative of social work, while admitting that the C.O.S. workers "may have to us an unpleasant odour of condescension, of hard-faced middle class women 'organizing' that lovely, elusive virtue of charity, of the 'haves' complacently denying help to the 'have nots,' " nevertheless wishes us to realize "how much the old C.O.S. achieved."

> Its discovery, repeating in a measure those of earlier times was that, if almsgiving is to be effective in helping the receiver rather than solacing the emotions of the giver, it must follow upon objective study of the situation which creates the need, and must be combined with a personal, individual approach in which everyone concerned is aiming at the same result. In modern terminology this would mean a thorough diagnosis followed by treatment planned in the light of diagnosis. This, for the C.O.S. pioneers involved the study of a variety of social situations as well as of individual need. (1964, p. 16)

14

Social philosophy aside, there is some evidence that the Young-husband analysis foreshortens the record in reading modern definitions of casework into the efforts of the C.O.S. Later, she adds: "Perhaps it would be true to say that for many years of its history it laid a greater emphasis on the organization of charity than on personal service and the rehabilitation of those in distress, but all the same its path lay in the line of a great tradition" (p. 25).

Richard M. Titmuss, Professor at the London School of Economics and Political Science, in a paper on "The Relationship between Schools of Social Work, Social Research, and Social Policy" (1964/1965), claims: "The historical evidence now available shows that the Charity Organization Society in England exercised a profound influence on poor law policies eighty years ago—much more powerful, though it was privately conducted and unsupported by research, than the effective influence of most schools of social work in the world today" (p. 69).

Whatever the influence on poor law policy exerted by the C.O.S., one may conclude with Younghusband: "The mistake they [the C.O.S.] made was in thinking that financial or other aid was in its nature calculated to undermine independence so that few should receive it and those few be subject to individual diagnosis and personal supervision" (1964, p. 16).

Other Ancestors

In time, the C.O.S. "passed over the water to the United States. In the last quarter of the nineteenth century we gave to them the C.O.S. and we and they together 'discovered' probation and the settlement movement" (Younghusband, 1964, p. 18).

If modern social work is not eager to associate itself with Loch or the less appealing characteristics of the C.O.S. founders, there is as little reason to include certain other ancestors in its family tree.

We may dismiss St. Vincent de Paul as not being in direct line with the C.O.S. The heroic personal charity of the saint who was consumed with the plight of the galley criminal seems to be essentially of a different order from the principles of Charles Stewart Loch, who made the C.O.S., and, in many ways, was the C.O.S. The founder of the 17th-century Daughters of Charity for work with the sick poor is representative of a different time, style, and spirit.

Octavia Hill, pioneer of sanitary reform and slum housing projects, sometimes mentioned as a founder of the C.O.S., essentially placed her hope not in the change of circumstances, nor in schemes or systems, but in a strong personal influence.

As for the probation movement, "we" is not to be interpreted as being connected with the C.O.S. John Augustus, a Boston bootmaker, is credited with first using the word "probation" in its modern

15

correctional sense in 1841, at the age of 57. His British counterpart was Matthew Davenport Hill of Birmingham, who pioneered something of the same nature, in the same year. Augustus died some 10 years prior to the founding of the C.O.S. (Dressler, 1965, pp. 11–18).

Finally, the *De subventione pauperum sive de humanis necessitatibus* of Juan Luis Vives, Spanish humanist, educator, and psychologist, published in 1526, often has been cited as inspiring the enactment of Tudor legislation to benefit the poor. This account of an experiment in dealing with poverty by municipal action, undertaken at Ypres in 1525, appeared in English translation in 1535. As far as ancestral connections to the C.O.S., it seems safe to conclude that the influence of Vives on Poor Law legislation may have been exaggerated ("Poor Law," 1966, p. 221).

Whatever their similarities in classifying the poor, the Poor Law and the C.O.S. were not coextensive. The C.O.S. originally sought to concentrate on "the deserving," leaving the others to the penal Poor Law. When such a line of demarcation proved impracticable, either because a confident judgment of deserving or undeserving could be made only in a small proportion of extreme cases, or because the needs of the deserving could not be met by the resources of the C.O.S., the Society dropped its original criterion for aid. The "helpable" patient now became the object of attention (Webb, 1926, pp. 195–196). "The one door opened by these 'friends of the poor' to all those they were unable to help privately, deserving as well as undeserving, was that of the workhouse with its penal discipline 'according to the principles of 1834' " (p. 196).

Woodroofe (1962) concludes that the sentiments of individuals such as General Booth, Canon Barnett, and Edward Denison "must have influenced quite profoundly the friendly visitors and social workers of the C.O.S." (p. 59). None of these, however, adds anything new to the basic position of the C.O.S., nor stands out as a significant genetic mutation regarding the place of the poor in society.

Edward Denison, cited as a founder of the C.O.S., disapproved of public works, referring to them as " 'that vortex of public works which leads inevitably to the bottomless pit of Communism' " (Woodroofe, 1962, p. 59, n. 2). Charity itself, he said, " 'is a frightful evil,' " in response to Octavia Hill's concern over what " 'our impatient charity is doing to the poor of London' " (Woodroofe, 1962, p. 26).

Chalmers's short-lived experiment in relief to the poor in Scotland in the early 19th century was characterized by individualized treatment, imaginative pursuit of resources, and automatic recruitment of the parish clergy into service. The accent on efficiency and economy of administration, and the belief that the beneficiary's character also would be improved, led indirectly to the charity organization movement and the creation of the London Charity Organization Society (Klein, 1968, pp. 148–149). Another "quite different" source was more responsible for a sympathetic approach, according to Klein: the efforts of Edward Denison, Arnold Toynbee, and the settlement movement (p. 149).

Canon Barnett accepted a "practicable" socialism, which he believed could be put into operation without revolution, redistribution of income, increase in taxation, or new political parties (Woodroofe, 1962, pp. 58, 59, 67).

Beatrice Webb (1926) observed: "The break-away of Samuel and Henrietta Barnett in 1886 from the narrow and continuously hardening dogma of the Charity Organization Society sent a thrill through the philanthropic world of London" (p. 200).

Without recanting their earlier denunciation of indiscriminate charity, the Barnetts had discovered for themselves, during their 12 years of residence in the extreme poverty of London's East End, that a deeper and more continuous evil existed—"namely, unrestricted and unregulated capitalism and landlordism" (Webb, 1926, p. 200). In short, the Barnetts had become aware of the employment of labor at starvation wages; of unsanitary tenements; and of the absence of opportunities for education, leisure, and the enjoyment of nature, art, and literature "among the denizens of the mean streets" (p. 200).

Without becoming socialists, in either the academic or the revolutionary sense, the Barnetts did initiate or further a long series of socialist measures, involving increased public expenditure and administration. According to Webb, it was Samuel Barnett's advocacy, in 1883, of universal state-provided old-age pensions which influenced Charles Booth.

Barnett did not advocate many changes in the law but wanted to see some of the best things in life made free: more baths, swimming facilities, books, pictures (Webb, 1926, p. 201).

Beatrice Webb saw "this nineteenth-century saint" (p. 202) as not wholly representative of the mid-Victorian spirit. "He carried over some of the mysticism of what we are apt to call 'primitive Christianity'; an overwhelming faith in the validity of the dominant impulse of the Christ and the Buddha; beneficence towards all human beings irrespective of their characteristics" (p. 204).

For all that, the embroidered and framed "One by One" motto which hung in the Barnetts' Toynbee Hall drawing room more nearly characterized the spirit of the settlement house workers than did the thrust of social inquiry. Mrs. Barnett is said to have spoken to her clients as though she expected them to obey swiftly. Indeed, it may have been her image of social work that inspired J. R. Green's savage satire of the social worker as a dictatorial busybody who retreated only before the Sister of Mercy or the Deaconess (Woodroofe, 1962, pp. 70–71).

The group activities movement initiated in England by Toynbee

Hall was continued in the settlement houses of the United States. Despite the efforts of modern social workers to give group work techniques coordinate status with those of casework, however, group work is practically nonexistent in social work theory. The settlement movement appears to have had little effect on the emergence of casework, whose most direct line of succession was the charity organization movement (Klein, 1968, pp. 172, 149).

Well into the modern era, professional social workers have remained loyal to the principle enunciated by Loch, long-time secretary of the C.O.S.: " 'Good casework is the first condition of organization' " (Woodroofe, 1962, p. 42).

If one sees the beginnings of modern casework in the early efforts of the C.O.S., one must look beyond the C.O.S. for the 19th-century origins of group work: to the Settlements, the YMCA and YWCA, the various boys' clubs, the Friendly Societies, and the Ragged Schools.

When the C.O.S. initiative crossed the Atlantic,

> American social work, like its English counterpart, was an integral part of the liberal's answer to life under a system of free enterprise. Both began as an attempt to temper the cold wind of capitalism to the shorn lamb of a proletariat whose existence was both a rebuke and a threat to the more fortunate class, and although in both countries social work changed as the framework of the existing social philosophy changed, the mark of the mint still remained. (Woodroofe, 1962, pp. 91-92)

Social work in America, with roots deep in 19th-century individualism, stressed individuality even more than in England. The doctrine that poverty was due to individual failure and that the poor could be divided into the deserving and the undeserving found ready agreement among a people who still cherished the log-cabin-to-White-House dream (p. 92).

The Charity Organisation Society, then, however well-intentioned its motives and whatever its advances over unorganized philanthropy, did not come to an understanding of poverty and its effects on the poor. That understanding, as well as the realization of the need for social organization, came from 19th-century men and women who were not the philosophical relatives of modern social workers.

Admittedly, social work's founders were not alone in their lack of perception: they shared the general valuations of the 19th century. However, there were other perspectives and options, which the C.O.S. did not pursue, and these deserve attention, beyond vague references to the three streams of human endeavor that emerged to meet the problems of the 19th century. These three streams, which "usually pursued their separate paths, eyeing each other with mistrust and sometimes with active hostility," were individual service, social and economic reform, and mutual aid, the last more closely related to social reform than to the personal service movement (Younghusband, 1964, pp. 25–26).

18

19TH-CENTURY ALTERNATIVES

There were several paths which the Charity Organisation Society chose not to take in its founding principles and its work with the poor during the 19th century. The Society's choices were not surprising: economic liberalism was the prevailing philosophy until the last quarter of the century. Nevertheless, C.O.S.'s choices were influential in setting the tone of the social work profession.

Writing of the pervasiveness of the Charity Organisation approach, Klein (1968) sees it as "a curious fact" that, in the period preceding the first steps toward establishing a school of social work in the United States, there seems to have been little interest in determining the seriousness and extensiveness of poverty and destitution—how many families actually lived on the brink of starvation.

> Aside from the few prophets like Jacob Riis, any thought given to the problem was in the channel and mold of charity organizations. It was quasi-scientific and efficiency-minded. Without quite saying so, it categorized the beneficiaries as a sort of permanent layer of helpless people, not too important except as a field of charitable, sympathetic, clear-headed, earnest philanthropists, but not for militant action. (pp. 222–223)

It is on the question of social organization, notably of the poor, that a radical distinction exists between the C.O.S. and several other options available in the 19th century. This central question also serves to cut off from the family tree of the C.O.S. a number of other men and women who have been philosophical ancestors to modern social thought.

To blunt the significance of social work's initial choice is to miss some significant implications of the profession's present dilemma.

Younghusband's (1964) analysis is optimistically superficial. In speaking of those three streams of social endeavor which originally "flowed in their separate courses, to the impoverishment of all of them," she concludes that "only now in the last decade or so . . . [are they] beginning to come together as we realize that though different they are not mutually exclusive ways of coming to grips with social problems" (p. 26).

The C.O.S. disliked the Fabians, who in turn disliked the C.O.S. because they fell into the opposite error of thinking that to cure economic ills and to offer certain universal services would of itself cure most individual problems of social maladjustment. In the end both were right and both were wrong. But alas! they failed to communicate with each other, and hence some of the troubles of the present day. (p. 16)

The differences between options was not simply a matter of dislike, nor of each choice being equally right and wrong at the same time.

If "the way ahead . . . lies in the alliance of sociology, psychiatry, social work and administration" (United Nations, 1958, p. 120), the original choices and their consequences must be more clearly delineated.

There is a considerable difference between the points of view that would see: (a) good casework as the antidote to Bolshevism, which the Society did as late as 1927; and (b) socialism or sociology as the antidote, as some British intellectuals of the 19th century hoped.

The Two Nations

The historical conditions and tensions in London at the inception of modern social work are interesting on two accounts: as the setting for the origin of the C.O.S., and as a parallel to political conditions and social welfare tensions in the United States during the 1930s, 1960s, and to some degree even today.

When the C.O.S. met to evolve a third method of dealing with poverty in a Victorian world of abundance, England was leading its rivals in the industrial race, and London was the financial center of something approaching a world economy. Victorians were satisfied with what they had become, and Woodroofe (1962) sees their faith in progress as based on complacent expectations that they would become even more like themselves in the future. "Their zest sometimes sprang from enthusiasm for sheer size and quantity—bigger population, more tons of coal, larger lines of railroads . . . but more often it was an excited tribute to that mastery over the physical universe" (p. 5).

However, the existence of another London, like Michael Harrington's *The Other America* (1962), was not to be denied.

Friedrich Engels had already become a socialist because of his revulsion at the working-class conditions in his native Rhineland and in England. He had already written *The Condition of the Working Class in England* in 1844, describing a class system in which labor was sold as a commodity. The work had attracted the attention of Karl Marx, who was to gain concrete understanding of working-class misery from his association and collaboration with Engels. The two had since collaborated on *The Communist Manifesto* (1848).

Manchester, wrote Engels, " 'is peculiarly built so that a person may live in it for years, and go in and out daily without coming into contact with a working-people's quarter or even with workers' " (Woodroofe, 1962, p. 7). General Booth's "denizens in darkest England" lived in conditions conveniently removed from the sight of Engels's "happier class" (pp. 6–7).

Benjamin Disraeli had described the existence of *The Two Nations* in 1845. Surveys and warnings on the conditions of the poor––by Sir Thomas Bernard, 1796; by Sir Freɔeric Morton Eden, 1797; and by Henry Mayhew, 1861, in which he described the plight of London's poor as being as little known as that of the pygmies of Africa—had increased Victorian fears of the underprivileged masses and their threat to the existence of private property.

Eden, owner of an insurance company, contributed three volumes on the social conditions of the working class. His series of working-class budgets, depressing as they were, were interpreted to prove that improvidence rather than lower wages was the cause of working-class poverty (Pfautz, 1967, p. 12).

One of the founders of *Punch*, Mayhew explicitly began his four-volume study to show that the condition of the poor "amidst all the immense wealth and great knowledge of 'the first city in the world,' is, to say the very least, a national disgrace to us" (1861–1862/1968, p. xvi). Inventing "oral history" a century before the term came into use, Mayhew assembled and codified thousands of pages of testimony from the poorest and least respectable denizens of London's streets. He earned the praise of William Thackeray for a picture of human life that surpassed in sheer drama the offerings of the novelists. Yet, novels such as Charles Dickens's *Bleak House* and *Our Mutual Friend*, as well as official publications like *The Report on the Sanitary Conditions of the City of London for the Years 1848–49*, also served to alert thoughtful Londoners to the problems of urbanization and rapid population growth.

But it remained for Charles Booth, three years before the New York C.O.S. started what later became the New York School of Social Work, to invent the social survey and to make what Beatrice Webb called "the grand inquest into the condition of life and labor of the four million inhabitants of the richest city in the world" (1926, p. 209), with the publication in 1889 of the first of 17 volumes of his *Life and Labour of the People in London* (1902–1903).

A man of means, like Bernard and Eden, Booth had the advantage over his predecessors of having available the results of the first census of 1801 and the subsequent censuses of 1881 and 1891. He also had the advantage of coming to see the problem of the poor in a new way, as a new evil—namely, as the result of urban squalor pro-

21

duced by increasing industrialization. By 1851, 50% of the population of England and Wales was classified as urban. At the time of Booth's writing, the percentage of urbanites had increased to 72%.

Booth did not survey the "poor" but turned his attention to a survey of "poverty." In an attempt to enlist support for his ambitious study, he wrote a "cryptic" outline of its general purpose: " 'to connect poverty and wellbeing with conditions of employment.' " He chose only " 'incidentally' " to describe the industrial peculiarities of London and modern towns generally, the character of work and workers, and the influences which acted on both (Pfautz, 1967, p. 23; Simey, 1960, p. 79).

In London of the 1890s, Booth was to find that 30.1% of the city's inhabitants lived at or below the level of poverty. Later, using more sophisticated techniques, he was to conclude that 31.5% of the city's population was below the poverty line.

What is important about Booth's 17-year study is his approach to the facts, an approach quite new to the 19th century. "The majority of Booth's countrymen preferred their individualism unlaced with socialism" (Woodroofe, 1962, p. 14).

Of particular interest is that Booth started out with essentially the same values as those of the first founders of social work. The difference lay in Booth's monumental pursuit of the fact and his enthusiasm for the positivism of Auguste Comte, founding father of sociology—who offered still another alternative to the solution of 19th-century problems and anxieties.

Booth was acquainted with C.S. Loch, founder of the C.O.S., as well as with Canon Barnett, founder of Toynbee Hall. Loch was originally enthusiastic about the prospects of Booth's proposed inquiry, though Canon Barnett doubted the possibility of his obtaining the data (Pfautz, 1967, p. 23).

Booth also was familiar with the propositions of the socialists, whose theories he regarded as "passionate suggestions of ignorance." In fact, it was Booth's desire to prove the socialists wrong in their theories and data, including their contention that fully 25% of London's workers received weekly wages on which it was impossible to live, that gave rise to a study which was to extend well beyond its projected three years.

In the end, the facts forced Booth to change his mind and to embrace a limited form of socialism, which he saw as a logical and efficient extension of the Poor Law.

> What is the Poor Law system? It is a limited form of Socialism—a Socialistic community (aided from the outside) living in the midst of an Individualist nation. . . . My idea is to make the dual system, Socialism in the arms of Individualism, under which we already live, more efficient by extending somewhat the sphere of the former and making the division of function more distinct. Our individualism fails because our Socialism is incomplete. (1902–1903, Vol. I, pp. 166–167)

22

Booth saw the necessity for a new solution: "I think that some-day the individualist community on which we build our faith, will find itself obliged for its own sake to take charge of the lives of those who, from whatever cause, are incapable of independent existence up to the required standard, and will be fully able to do so" (1888, p. 299).

In short, reform programs in the 19th century were not locked into one single option, not even that of the C.O.S., which Booth later was to criticize. Booth had some of the same motives and values as Loch: economic liberalism, the belief that rational behavior was economic behavior, and the transference of the emotion of self-sacrificing service from God to man. He rejected communism and settled for "Socialism in the arms of Individualism."

Beatrice Potter Webb, who also moved to socialism, was the only one of the first supporters of Booth's project to participate in the final endeavor. She defined the survey as "A Grand Inquest into the Condition of the People of London" (1926, p. 209), and she was quite definite about the difference between Booth's work and the aims of the C.O.S., "my friend the enemy—the Charity Organization Society—one of the most typical of mid-Victorian social organizations" (p. 189).

In her years of apprenticeship with the C.O.S., from 1883 to 1887, "the C.O.S. appeared to me as an honest though short-circuited attempt to apply the scientific method of observation and experiment, reasoning and verification, to the task of delivering the poor from their miseries by the personal service and pecuniary assistance tendered by their leisured and wealthy fellow-citizens." These C.O.S. aims were based on prized mid-Victorian principles: "patient and persistent personal service on the part of the well-to-do; an acceptance of personal responsibility for the ulterior consequences, alike to the individual recipient and to others who might be indirectly affected, of charitable assistance; and finally . . . the application of the scientific method in each separate case of a damaged body or lost soul; so that the assistance given should be based on a correct forecast of what would actually happen, as a result of the gift, to the character and circumstances of the individual recipient and to the destitute class to which he belonged" (p. 190).

To Booth, however, poverty was not a part of the preordained natural order, nor proof of individual contrariness.

> It was not to be exorcized by incantations on thrift and self-help. It was human, explicable, and removable, and if the existing methods for dealing with it were inadequate, unsuitable or desultory, the State itself must step into the role of provider. (Woodroofe, 1962, p. 11)

Booth's plan for a welfare state was rejected, and the prevailing distrust of the poor continued to infuse the theory and practice of poor relief for some time.

The value tensions which existed when social work had its beginnings are still evident today, at a time when social work feels it has come of age. The late President John F. Kennedy delivered the first presidential speech in Congress on the subject of welfare, emphasizing that the nature and objectives of public assistance must change with changing times to meet human needs (Glover and Reid, 1964, p. 11).

America's largest child welfare program, AFDC, was failing to meet the needs of children, and in 1964 not all American states had taken advantage of the federal provision from AFDC payments to households with unemployed but employable fathers. The last of the major Western nations to establish a national program of social insurance and welfare, the United States in 1964 remained one of the few not providing financial support for families without a means test. While Western European countries were spending for social insurance a percentage of total national income three times greater than that of the United States, "our people have clung to the myth that every enterprising American can be self-supporting" (Glover and Reid, 1964, p. 11).

There were at least two broad social reform forces, two giant prongs, by which the 19th century attempted to lift itself above the social problems and perplexity caused by industrialization, the burgeoning growth of cities, and the poor. The first was the method of inquiry, including Auguste Comte's new science of sociology, seeking to establish a role position in a society institutionally convinced of the need and value of public service. The second was an ameliorism by the rich of the wretched conditions of the poor, a movement whose very success "aggravated the general perplexity" (Abrams, 1968, p. 52).

The culmination of the ameliorist movement was the establishment of the National Association for the Promotion of Social Science, which promoted social legislation in its annual congresses from 1857 to 1884 and which offered, through its publication *Meliora*, a piecemeal type of social science and a justification for the position that social science was utilitarian Christianity in action.

The Charity Organisation Society was one of 38 corporate bodies embraced under the NAPSS.

Indeed, the Charity Organisation Society was only *one*, if "an outstanding product of the movement of ameliorism."

> The vehemence with which the C.O.S. and its supporters reiterated the traditional moral sociology, "that character is nine-tenths of life," in the face of intensified social disorder in the 1880's, [when the NAPSS was already in difficulties] exacerbated the doubts of others. By reaction they were driven back to first principles—and to the possibility of new first principles. What was bad for the science of social reform was, if anything, good for sociology. (Abrams, 1968, p. 52)

As the C.O.S. was an outstanding product of the broad social force of ameliorism in Victorian England, sociology in Britain was an outstanding, if not immediately highly successful, product of the greater force of social inquiry.

Abrams points out that the history of British sociology before 1914, even before 1945, is in no way a success story. He begins the history of sociology in Britain in the 1830s, "when men first realized they were living in an industrial society," specifically in 1834, the year of the Report of the Commission on the Poor Law and the founding of the Statistical Society of London (p. 34 and Note).

In point of time, then, social work is slightly younger than (and related through one cultural parent to) the science of sociology, so named by Comte in the belief that the time had come to crown the achievements of the older sciences with a new queen—the positive science of the social order.

Sociology had difficulty establishing itself as a separate entity, not because of any scarcity of intelligent leadership, but because Victorian England offered so many different options as solutions to the problems of industrialization and urbanization.

Political action and public service on the part of the well-to-do were institutionalized. The Statistical Society, which Booth joined, offered one avenue of social inquiry. The theories of the economists, based on Adam Smith's "invisible hand," eventually proved to be not totally convincing, but economic activity was seen as another possible alternative.

The universities were busy with their own ideology, more Platonic than pragmatic or empirical, as Harry Elmer Barnes noted. There was a wide spectrum of amelioristic choices—quicker, more direct, and more immediately satisfying to the benevolent individual than was sociological analysis. And, of great importance, there were the patterned explanations of socialism and communism, offered as alternatives to small-scale measures and small-scale explanations.

As we have seen, it is important in understanding social work's beginnings to see the C.O.S. as one of the strands of a Victorian ameliorist tradition, rather than as a singularly apt evolutionary development of the Judeo-Christian ethic; it is equally important to see the fascinating complexity of alternative options within the broad thrust of social inquiry, and the part played by the developing science of sociology, to understand the persistent hate-love dependency that has characterized the relationship between modern social work and sociology.

If the two often have been mistaken as compatible kin, there is some historical reason for such an assumption: both disciplines emerged as a response to the same problem, within some 50 years of each other, and there were pioneers in both camps who moved back and forth across their noninstitutionalized boundaries. (Comte himself suffered some early rejection in Britain because of that part of his program which shared the amelioristic thrust of a religion of humanity in a uniquely Comtean vision.)

On the other hand, if the literature of social work gives evidence of incompatibility between the helping discipline and sociology, there is equally good historical justification. The roots of mutual mistrust lie in the radically different approaches of the two disciplines to the social problems of the 19th century. The effects of this divergence persisted as late as 1965 in such acknowledged epithets as old girls and new boys, true believers and iconoclasts, anti-intellectuals and irresponsible theorists, fuzzy-minded feelers and academic gamesmen—the second half of each dichotomy referring to social workers trained in research and the social sciences (Schubert, 1965, p. 42, n. 10).

Even Klein, discussing group work as a technique "that actually ... does not exist" in social work, feels constrained to add that "the semantic seduction of the social sciences has added to the problem" (1968, pp. 172–173).

There is much to be lost by social work's ambivalence toward sociology, especially when social work's most thorough self-examinations agree that it still must come to grips with the social sciences. Reading what social workers say of their own historical identity conveys the continuous impression that modern social workers miss what the C.O.S. missed, the point that the French father of sociology was writing to the spirit of the time "with an appealing voice to men oppressed by a sense of the fragmentation of knowledge and by their own inability to focus knowledge effectively for purposes of social action. And it was in that way that British intellectuals discovered him after 1873" (Abrams, 1968, p. 54).

Enthusiasm for Comte during his lifetime was limited to a small group; the abbreviated 1853 version of his *Positive Philosophy*, by Harriet Martineau, sold slowly. As late as 1870, Comte was known mainly through Mill's and Spencer's negative reactions to him.

> There is force to the argument, used by both Mill and Spencer, that much that was intellectually new about sociology in the 1870's sprang from the common scientific (positivist?) culture of the age in which Comte, too, was a participant. The demand for a science of society was rampant. To articulate the spirit of the age did not give one property rights to it. (Abrams, 1968, p. 55)

Nevertheless, certain central emphases of British sociology ultimately were to be Comtean. However abhorrent his Religion of Humanity was to the British, "Comte was seen to have done three things. He had defined a subject matter. He had demonstrated a method of analysis. And he had set out a program of moral education and political action" (Abrams, 1968, p. 55). Abrams notes that the tendency of British social scientists was to absorb the subject matter and the method, while repudiating the program, thus denying that they had been influenced by Comte.

Both the subject matter and the method of sociology—encompassing the entire social order—made sociology a radical theoretical opponent of the C.O.S.

In the summer of 1903, the Sociological Society of London was formed, the first such national association in Europe. Though it was not yet clear what sociology was to be—there were so many different brands of it (Abrams, 1968, p. 3)—its solution was not to be the solution of the C.O.S. By 1903, sociology was different enough from the tradition of the C.O.S. that its fervent secretary, C. S. Loch, "was already caught up in defending the Charity Organisation Society against newer views of the proper treatment of poverty" (pp. 104–105).

The various possibilities within sociology—Comte's, Spencer's, Le Play's sociology of social action (and one wonders why the last did not appeal to the C.O.S.)—were not the only alternatives available in the realm of social explanation. Sydney and Beatrice Webb were attracted to socialism, and for that reason should not be regarded among the pioneers of modern social work. The Eugenicists, like the sociologists, were concerned with rigorous empirical method, thanks largely to Francis Galton, the parent of modern statistical methods. However, they looked for the cure to society's ills in the explanation of racial disintegration, along the lines of Spencer and Darwin.

Thus, if social work today complains that it departed from the way of sociology because the latter did not establish scientific formulations to which social work practice could relate (Beck, 1959, p. 203), one can only sympathize with the difficult choices facing social pioneers in the face of conflicting social possibilities.

There were, nevertheless, pioneers in the social problems tradition who were led, as a result of social inquiry, to a position which might be called essentially sociological. One such pioneer was Charles Booth, who definitely is not in the C.O.S. social work tradition, despite his identification with social work by social workers. Mary E. MacDonald (1960) writes that the origins of social work research are lost in the origins of social work itself. If one thinks only of developing bodies of knowledge put to use by successive generations of professional social workers, "then the conclusion is inescapable that social work research has made a relatively slight contribution" (p. 6). Nevertheless, she includes as "precursors of social work research" (p. 5) Charles Booth; the English pioneer of prison reform, John Howard (1726–1790); and Sir Frederick Eden (1766–1806), who undertook to determine the state of the poor and the history of the poor law.

Eden's findings, to repeat, were interpreted in the economic-liberal perspective. However, Klein (1968) sees Eden's *State of the Poor* as a unique, almost prophetic work: the first attempt in 600 years of English history to gauge the extent and form of poverty in a scholarly way (p. 254). Eden's research spirit does not suggest kinship with social work's research efforts.

Howard, in his all-consuming pursuit of prison reform in Europe, also was considerably removed in time from the C.O.S. He is even further removed from the C.O.S. philosophy, however, by the single-minded pursuit and effectiveness of his prison investigation.

Booth included the Charity Organisation Society along with religious groups as evading rather than fulfilling, in their practical applications, many of the teachings set forth in the Bible (1902–1903, Vol. VII, p. 413).

Charles Booth was a pioneer in social problems who painstakingly arrived, through a process of changing his mind that began at age 47, at a new concept of poverty as not structurally inevitable.

As Abrams notes, in the crisis of the 1890s, when it became apparent that the social process of poverty had been studied hardly at all, British intellectuals turned instinctively to the pursuit of more and better empirical information, as they had done earlier in the century. "One possibility was socialism; another was sociology; there were many others" (Abrams, 1968, p. 85).

For men such as Hobhouse and Geddes, sociology was an alternative to social biology. "Sociology stood in a dialectical relationship to the tradition of Darwin and Spencer. Only when and if the errors of that tradition had been demonstrated would sociology, embodying a true understanding of social evolution, come into its own. Conversely, it was the errors of the social-biological tradition that made efforts to develop sociology so imperative" (Abrams, 1968, p. 90).

Abrams calls Booth the most influential product of this new dilemma of relevance to sociology, noting that "he did begin his work with the explicit intention of contributing new knowledge as well as new information" (p. 85).

So much, then, for Booth as a "precursor" of social work research.

Woodroofe (1962) concludes that the possibility that the plight of the poor resulted, wholly or in part, from the economic set-up of society "did not enter the collective mind of the C.O.S." To them, "character, not circumstance," was the cause of failure (p. 34).

To Loch, as to modern social workers generally, the family was seen as the perfect bastion of defense, and state public works were frowned upon. In the case of more modern social work efforts, governmental aid to needy families in the United States generally proceeded in spite of the profession.

Thus, "Loch issued grim warnings against 'the State as caterer-in-chief for its citizens.' " As late as 1905, the C.O.S. sternly denounced the Unemployed Workmen Act on the grounds that " 'what is called the problem of unemployment cannot be solved by the artificial provision of work with relief more or less disguised as wages' " (Woodroofe, 1962, p. 39).

Approving an assistance that was individual, personal, temporary, and reformatory—and which usually did not include paying back rent or funeral expenses—the Society often grossly underestimated the extent of the poverty with which the C.O.S. or the state had to deal.

On one occasion, Loch was so intent on defeating the proposals of Booth for an old-age pension of five shillings a week—as potentially pauperizing unfortunate recipients—that he could quote Giffen's figures on the jagged distribution of income between classes without realizing their significance. Despite Loch's protestations to the contrary, detection of fraud was an important part of the Society's work "and was a bait which attracted many followers to the C.O.S. banner" (Woodroofe, 1962, p. 43).

Whatever the early connections of the C.O.S. with sociology, and there were a few, the Charity Organisation Society's long, drawn out struggle with socialism continued, not with sociological insights, but, rather, with some of the most unsatisfying assumptions of the 19th century.

In the course of this struggle, social casework became identified with the Society's political and social philosophy. Thus, in 1927, the Fifty-Eighth Annual Report of the C.O.S. was titled "Bolshevism and Its Only True Antidote." The Report, with the fervent optimism of a Loch, asserted that " 'the only real antidote to Bolshevism is good casework' " (Woodroofe, 1962, p. 55).

1965: TOIL AND DOUBLE TROUBLE

Despite social work's heralded coming of age in 1965, there are considerable indications in discussions of the present state of social work knowledge that things are not as they should be.

According to Younghusband in "Forward to 1903," originally written in 1953, the high mark of British social work occurred some 34 years after the founding of the Charity Organisation Society (1964, p. 15). After that, the profession entered a dark age. "How promising and how full of vigour was social work in England fifty years ago!" she laments (p. 18).

After that high mark, when the C.O.S. started its own School of Sociology, an eclipse set in, "relieved only by two or three rays of light since the early days of the century" (p. 21).

> There in our history lies the challenge to us. Much that we had we blindly threw away or let slip, much that we could have had we ignored. Yet after all the years of marking time we have a chance once more to go forward, a chance better even than that of fifty years ago because of all the achievements in social welfare and scientific knowledge since those days. If, then, this is no time for complacency, yet it is a time for hope and effort, a time in which we can learn from the discoveries and the failure of the past in order to go forward and do that which is required of us in the future. (p. 22)

Younghusband is hopeful that social workers "have begun to see that in concentrating on some one particular aspect of the individual we have lost sight of him as a full human being who is part of a family and part of a network of social relationships, and that these come first in helping him to meet his deficiencies, instead of being the incidentals which we have made them" (pp. 21–22).

Though she feels the pendulum has not yet swung very far in practice, she sees "much heart-searching about our bewildering variety of specialized trainings." At last, she concludes, social work is beginning to realize "that the application of academic knowledge does not happen all of itself, and that in addition to the application of knowledge there is a skill in social work which needs guidance and teaching in order to produce it" (p. 22).

According to the *Third International Survey* (United Nations, 1958), social work in the United States continued along the lines of integrated theory and practice, absorbing material from the social and behavioral sciences and applying it in practice. Apparently, then, it is to social work in the United States that the international social work community looks for aid in its resurgence. "For some years now, social work education has been striving to recapture its lost early wisdom and to learn to apply, adapt and expand American methods and literature creatively in different social conditions and cultures" (United Nations, 1958, p. 119).

The period of early wisdom, it should be noted, was very brief, since, as we have seen, the straitlaced philosophy of the early Charity Organisation Society permeated British and American social work well into the 20th century.

The State of the Art in America

If the status of social work is bad in Britain, how much better is it in the United States, home of the younger branch of the social work profession? Social workers' statements about themselves and their profession may provide an answer.

At first glance, the reader is struck by the optimism of the American social work profession, which marked "Social Work's coming of age as a profession" with the launching, in the spring of 1965, of the *Journal of Education for Social Work*. Published by the professional accrediting agency, the Council on Social Work Education, the *Journal* is concerned exclusively with education for the field of social welfare in all its aspects: trends, new developments, and problems at the undergraduate, Master's, and post-Master's levels. The editors have selected manuscripts "by the criteria of relevance of their content to major issues in social work education, scholarly soundness in presentation, and promise of lasting interest to, and significance for, the field" (Council on Social Work Education, Spring 1965, Masthead).

Though the opinions expressed in the articles are those of the authors, nevertheless the Council introduces "with gratitude and pride the group of outstanding leaders in social welfare and in social work education who form our editorial advisory panel"—a panel that shows "concern with *mainstream issues* encountered in the educational preparation of social personnel at all levels and the contribution they make to the solution of pressing problems" (p. 3, italics added).

The Council's primary purpose in publishing the *Journal* "is to help us all keep abreast of the forward thrust of thinking and program innovation in social work education and in related fields" (Council on Social Work Education, Fall 1965, p. 2).

Quite obviously, what the Council thinks, as reflected in its selection of contributors, eminently suggests what schools of social work are likely to think, and what students of social work are likely to be taught. Any other opinions are in a minority position, since schools need accreditation just as students need degree credentials. In 1965, the Council supervised the educational offerings of some 75 graduate professional schools of social work in the United States and Canada, with 209 affiliated undergraduate departments.

A Content Analysis

The buoyancy of the initial presentation in the *Journal* is at some odds with conclusions drawn from a content analysis of the first year and a half of publication—a total of three issues. The content analysis suggests that the *Journal* does not "reaffirm hard-won advances in social work education," but instead is saying substantially what Younghusband concluded about social work in England:

> Up till now we (both practising social workers and those concerned with their training) have done depressingly little to help ourselves. Others have laboured and we have not even entered into their labours. Other people indeed have done a good deal more for us than we have done for ourselves. Almost all the literature we have is produced either by non-social workers in this country or else by social workers on the other side of the Atlantic; we have got almost nowhere with supervision as a means of relating class room teaching to field work practice in order to help students to develop social work skill; and we have not collected the material nor done the hard thinking needed to teach social work at a proper academic level. Consequently we social workers are not being used as we might be used, achieving what we might achieve, advancing as we might advance, and this not because other people fail to recognize our merits but because we ourselves stagnate at a low level of achievement, whether academically, or in practice or social action. (1964, p. 22)

If social workers in England are looking to their American counterparts for integrated theory and practice, the *Journal* gives substantial evidence that such hopes are misplaced.

Content analysis of major themes has some limitations, but there is no other objective way to penetrate the characteristic social work style of presentation: an amalgam of unsupported optimism, circular discussion, and devastating criticism and self-recrimination, not only within the same article, but often within a few paragraphs.

Granting the tendency of professional groups to perennial self-examination, nevertheless one must conclude that, if even half of the questions raised in the first three issues of the *Journal* remain to be answered, the dream of Loch has not been met almost 100 years later. Social work has not become increasingly scientific.

The editors of the *Journal* start off by summarizing briefly the problems facing the profession (Council on Social Work Education,

Spring 1965, pp. 2–3). These casually cited problems can be grouped into six general areas which, with their subhead areas, encompass the philosophy, content, methods, and manpower dilemmas of the entire profession. According to the editors, however, "these are but a few of the questions before us."

The six general problem areas include: (1) the appropriateness of the direction and emphases of graduate education in view of today's social needs; (2) a lack of knowledge regarding social work's student body and the extent to which admission policies are screening in or out particular student types; (3) doubts about the quality and competence of social work faculty; (4) disagreement about the essentials of the curriculum in social work education, including desirable undergraduate preparation; (5) questions about the adequacy of professional education for public social service and voluntary agencies; and (6) the need for cooperation with social work education in other countries, as well as for cooperation with other disciplines.

In 1959, Wootton criticized the arrogance of the language with which social workers describe their activities. She stated that the description of social work activity generally does not match the activity actually performed by social workers. "Happily, also, the literature of social work is not generally read by those who receive its administration. Without doubt the majority of those who engage in social work are sensible, practical people, who conduct their business on a reasonably matter-of-fact basis. The pity is that they have to write such nonsense about it" (p. 279).

How well social workers do their work, despite how unrealistically they write, actually is the subject of another survey. The pity of it, in my opinion, is that, to do good work, the student of social work must forget most of what has been learned in the academic social work curriculum—not only to survive the academic effects of the Master's or graduate degree, but, possibly more important, to survive the undeniable *mystique* of the socializing process whereby recruits are turned into helping people on a professional level.

This seems a great waste of time, especially when we admit we are doing badly in this area and there still is so much to be learned. From the standpoint of a beginning sociology of social work, what we encounter early in the journey into social work's past is a history that does not explain and a socializing experience that does not prepare one to cope effectively.

One of the first marks of the social work *mystique* is the very style of the profession's literature; it is a quasi-scientific monologue that has severed connections with the academic precision and standards of proof usually urged, admittedly often without success, upon college freshmen. The voluminous literature of social work is notably lacking in sustained discussion on single issues. Consequently, the student or other reader is confronted with a continuous reinforcement of the same ideas and methods, which, though criticized in moments of candor, continue to be quoted ritualistically as substantiation of their worth or of the worth of other ideas.

Obviously, this literature is a pervasive influence on students, especially as social workers claim a special social work knowledge, from which heretics are easily excommunicated.

The content analysis which follows is intended to serve as an introduction to that literature, in greatly abbreviated form to make for easier reading. The object has been to locate statements about key social work positions from which a more extended backward and forward survey might be made.

It should be noted that it is possible to examine other disciplines and piece together almost equally negative assessments, though probably not in so few issues of an accreditation agency's official journal. In this case, however, the subject is social work and its present state of knowledge and technique.

The assumption behind this analysis is that whenever and wherever there is widespread criticism and dissatisfaction within a discipline, these can serve as the beginnings of new movements and options. As such, criticism and dissatisfaction are the hopeful signs that, although theory is theory and practice is practice, at some point, as David Dressler observes, they should come together—especially for social workers, who deal in applied science.

Whether, in fact, social worker dissatisfaction gives evidence of being a harbinger of change is a question we shall examine later in this analysis.

Theoretical Base

What does social work know? Briefly, in terms of the theory from which social work draws its applied art, practically nothing.

Two "significant" problems in the master's degree program in social work education "call for the critical attention of all social work educators": the level and the nature of the professional content (Kadushin, 1965, p. 33). "Restating the problem in the most direct and least compassionate way, social work education is postbaccalaureate education; although it leads to a professional degree, it is not graduate education" (p. 34).

Social work education is advanced education only in a temporal sense: it follows four years of college. The profession does not build on a common body of knowledge, which all incoming students can be expected to have mastered. As a result, although "it is graduate-level in point of time, it is still undergraduate education in terms of profundity, complexity, and rigor of content" (p. 34).

This problem of lack of content extends beyond the classroom into the field—that locus of social work education and activity which uniquely defines what social workers do and tests the skill potential and sincerity of aspirants for a profession of doing rather than thinking about doing. Students who show some dissatisfaction with current field methods ordinarily are suspected of rejecting the calling.

Social Work Methods

The problem of content is not confined to social work education alone: "it affects the entire field of social work. It is a problem of direction" (Kadushin, 1965, p. 41). There are signs within the profession of a growing disenchantment with what psycho-therapeutically-oriented casework, the profession's first and most developed method, can do for people who need help.

> Intensive casework, psychotherapy, counseling—whatever it may be called—has by now, had opportunity to prove itself. There is more than a suspicion that, at best, it is a resource which is applicable to only a limited segment of the potential client group, that to be a "good" casework client demands of most people personality attributes, motivation, and orientation which few of them possess. (p. 41)

This problem of content is seen as a "dismal but accurate picture. . . . in any of the practice methods by which social work seeks to achieve its ultimate aims, professional social workers must function with a body of knowledge that at best is imprecise, at worse is erroneous and always is inadequate and difficult to communicate" (M. Burns, 1965, pp. 13–14).

A review of the current state of social work knowledge "discloses a devastating lack of agreement as to the definitions of many of the concepts in use." Frames of reference are vague and general; theories are either too general or too limited to be applicable. Middle-level theory is largely missing. "Practice knowledge has been only inadequately codified and practice wisdom is largely unvalidated" (M. Burns, 1965, p. 13).

We find the social worker lacking clear definitions for such commonly used concepts as insight, group bond, grass roots community organization, and ego strengths. "This lack of conceptual clarity is present in all of the practice methods and pervades much of the content in the areas of social services and human behavior, upon which operational theory draws heavily." One of the most pressing needs of the profession is "to clean up the constructs" (M. Burns, 1965, pp. 14, 16).

Compounding the basic problem of knowledge building in social work is a lack of qualified persons within the profession to undertake the task. This problem was raised in the House of Delegates discussion at the Council of Social Work Education's Thirteenth Annual Program Meeting (M. Burns, 1965, p. 17).

Core Content

The basic "core content" of the first stage of preparation for responsible entrance into social work education remains unidentified. "We have not yet sufficiently identified and formulated this 'core,' " but such a core "must certainly include familiarity with current learning theory and a working competence with the concept Bruner calls 'structure' of a subject—a grasp of the underlying structure or significance of complex knowledge, even to the degree that learning properly under optimum conditions enables one to 'learn how to learn' " (Blackey, 1965, pp. 8–9).

Previous efforts at conceptualization and generalization of knowledge and experience in professional social work have been "valiant," but insufficient to produce a general understanding of the structure of the subject matter at the level indicated by Bruner. Social work, however, now sees an opportunity to experiment with methods of teaching fundamental structure effectively; to provide learning conditions to foster such teaching; to develop curricula as effective vehicles for this knowledge; to know more about learners generally and social work learners in particular; to acquire knowledge and skills essential for working with groups of learners; and to become familiar with the resources for teaching, the various media, and the methodologies most appropriate to social work's goal (Blackey, 1965, p. 9).

The Problem of Research

Neither the search for theory nor declamations on its urgency are new in social work. Geis contends that the acquisition of knowledge currently required by social work would take more years than social work can afford to wait. "But it is just as true that, had we undertaken such investigation at the proper time, we would not be so painfully ignorant today. And if we do not begin now to conduct sophisticated studies of the 'if-then' consequences of various forms of education for social work, we will be no more informed (or less misinformed) in another decade than we are presently" (Geis, 1965, p. 28).

There is a good deal of repetition in the profession's lament over the lack of clear theory and objective practice criteria. Nearly 50 years ago, Edith Abbott (1931) complained that it is "in part because our field has been neglected by the scholar that progress has often been so lamentably slow." She quoted approvingly Toynbee's suggestion that "to make benevolence scientific is the great problem of the present day" (Geis, 1965, p. 28, n. 7; Abbott, 1931, p. 2).

As early as 1951, Hollis and Taylor, in their comprehensive survey of social work education, pointed to the need for systematic study of social work theory and practice. The authors predicted difficulty in determining the character, amount, and distribution of educational facilities if such research were not undertaken (Geis, 1965, p. 28; Kadushin, 1965, p. 35; see Hollis and Taylor, 1951, pp. 96–97).

In 1959, the massive Curriculum Study sponsored by the Council on Social Work Education seconded the recommendation of an earlier study that an undergraduate-graduate continuum of educational requirements be established. This suggestion, frequently advanced, has never really been implemented (Kadushin, 1965, p. 35; see Boehm, 1959).

By 1964, Dean Mossman concluded at the annual program meeting that enough is now known "about levels of practice and given educational programs to set up some well-planned exploratory studies" (Geis, 1965, p. 28).

The Problem of Field Work

"One of the greatest obstacles to developing social work practice theory," according to Margaret Schubert (1965), is that "there is no simple, straightforward, objective, and at the same time valid, measure of successful treatment. The absence of a clear-cut measure of success has consequences for research in practice, for public understanding, for teaching, and for practice itself" (p. 39).

As noted by Robert Vinter in 1963, one consequence of the lack of theory, and the consequent difficulty of assessing results, is that professional behavior tends to become valued for its own sake. "This is not to say that the profession wallows in total ignorance or that 'professional behavior' is valueless; but that professional knowledge in social work is incomplete, and some of the professional behavior that is taught in field work may prove to be ineffective" (Schubert, 1965, p. 39).

In a recent study of theses in psychiatric settings dealing with various aspects of mental illness and the family, Elizabeth McBroom (1965) found the use of psychodynamic theory by one group of students to be "adequate . . . though somewhat distorted by overextension, with lack of social perspectives, ethnic group differentiations, and governing class norms of families studied" (p. 31). Despite the obvious lack of social understanding on the part of these students, McBroom uses the study's results as evidence that knowledge about the person has been "best developed and best presented" in the traditional behavior courses (p. 30).

The research interviews showed an ability on the part of students to help respondents relate to a research purpose and reveal feelings in well-defended areas. "This confirms much contemporary professional self-criticism: that the knowledge base lags behind clinical skills and sensitivity. Practitioners have had to do better than they know. But the field is beginning to operate on the conviction that practice can be made more consistently effective by extension and systematic teaching of the knowledge base" (p. 31).

Perspective and Values

According to William Gordon (1965), "social work is an evolving profession, still in the process of construction" (p. 20). Over the past 10 or 15 years, however, "it has become obvious that the field of social work has a perspective of its own awaiting theoretical development" (p. 19).

The articulation of this social work frame of reference has become, according to Gordon, not only possible but "imperative." In an "attempt to begin this articulation, at least to the extent of contributing to the vitality and usefulness of the term," he notes that there is "cogent evidence for the existence of some commonalities which cut across these idiosyncratic variations, a perspective we share as members of the profession." At the same time, however, he expresses concern over the considerable variation in individual perspectives and, therefore, in the particular frame of reference used by each social worker (p. 19).

As of 1965, then, social work's theoretical framework still awaits articulation. Even more chastening to a belief in the inevitability of progress is the realization that Loch's dream of increasingly scientifically trained workers motivated by the religion of humanity has not been attained on the latter score any more than on the former.

The special volume on *Values and Ethics* of the 1959 Curriculum Study (Pumphrey, 1959) concluded that not enough is known about values to be conclusive. In summary, the 164-page report said: "Not only was there general vagueness as to the exact kind of value behavior required in social work practice but also there appeared to be a dearth of information in related social science fields which could suggest from previous research how to go about seeking the answers" (p. 4).

There are, in fact, strong similarities of thrust and optimism between Loch's 1904 apologia for entering the C.O.S. and the rallying cry of the new American *Journal*. Said Loch in 1904:

> "I should answer that through its work and growth I hoped that some day there would be formed a large association of persons drawn from all churches and classes who, disagreeing in much, would find in charity a common purpose and a new unity. ... It could make legislation effective, could see that it was enforced. Apart from all legislative interference and with the use of means and influences more far-reaching it could renew and discipline the life of the people by a nobler, more devoted, more scientific religious charity. It could turn to account all that newer knowledge would bring to the help of charity. It could even-

tually provide out of all classes and sects a great array of friendly and by degrees well-trained workers. It could help us to realise in society the religion of charity without the sectarianism of religion." (Woodroofe, 1962, pp. 31–32)

The *Journal of Education for Social Work* declared in 1965:

For social work education, "the time is now" to carry into its study, debate, and analysis the belief that caring in a responsible way about people it is the privilege of our profession to serve means becoming deeply involved in learning how to serve them better, with vastly more scientific acumen and with a steadily deepening body of knowledge and increased artistry in its use. (Spring 1965, p. 3)

By 1965, two major elements were being explored for their potential in focusing and developing the value system of social work and "building its expertise—that is, for developing its science." First, as a central value, "social work should assume unequivocally that it is good for every individual to develop—to realize—the most of his potential for growth in the broadest sense of both words: 'potential' and 'growth' " (Gordon, 1965, p. 22).

The second major element assumes some acknowledgment of the social worker's area of competence, which "lies somewhere in the pattern of man's social functioning, or coping with his environment, as it enhances or inhibits his realization and contributes to or detracts from the environmental medium for his and others' developments of their potentials" (p. 22).

"The clearer focusing on realization of the human potential as a central value is not new in the world or unique to social work," notes Gordon. "It is only beginning, however, to be seen as a serious goal, even in social work" (p. 22).

Criteria of Relevance

" 'How relevant is relevant?' So persistent is this question throughout social work education," reports Bess Dana (1965), that "it has been identified by the schools as a major issue for consideration by the Council's Curriculum Committee" (p. 6).

Finding social work's knowledge base and then translating it into the curriculum is, according to Dana, a "Herculean" task. "The embarrassment of riches with which the social work educator today is faced, as new theories about man and society replace or cast shadows of uncertainty on the old," forces the question of relevance onto the profession (p. 6).

Casework

There is disenchantment within the profession with casework, social work's primary and most developed method, not only because of its limitation to certain situations, but because of its limitations even within those situations.

Even moving from an emphasis on helping the client develop a greater ability to cope with stress (the psychotherapeutic approach favored in the past) to a greater emphasis on reducing the stress with which the client has to cope . . . maneuverability is limited. The real social deprivations which so many clients face—poor housing, structural unemployment, discrimination, marginal assistance budgets, limited income, low educational attainment, limited marketable skills, etc.—stem from situations over which neither the worker nor the client has any individual control. (Kadushin, 1965, pp. 42–43)

The difficulty encountered by those with the least ego strength in trying to meet the demands of psychotherapeutic casework has led to intensive casework being described as a process of "saving the saved. . . . While Cloward accuses social work of 'planned disengagement' from offering services to the 'poor'—historically social work's rightful clientele—it is just as true to say that the 'poor' have abandoned social work as it has developed" (p. 41).

Group Work

Essentially the same criticism that is leveled at casework—that it is not meeting the needs of the client—can be extended to traditional group work as well, "with perhaps somewhat less justification" (Kadushin, 1965, p. 42, n. 38).

Community Organization

Growing recognition of the limitations of casework has resulted in increasingly frequent requests for a de-emphasis of casework in the curriculum to permit greater emphasis on other approaches, notably community organization. "There is no dearth of resolutions proposed for many social problems. . . . The rub is in effecting these necessary changes. Discouragement over how far social work can go in this direction is based on familiarity with the limited repertory of principles available to teach regarding how a community can be helped to change" (p. 43).

Community organization, the profession's third and least developed traditional method, remains on a "primitive" level (McBroom, 1965, p. 32).

The key problem is that nobody has yet been able to operationalize social change theory and create a method that could be used by practitioners in an effort to alter social systems and structures. It is all very well, therefore, to say to social workers that they should shift their focus from individual change to social change, but unless one builds onto current knowledge of acts of intervention new acts which constitute a professional process to induce social change, social workers may cheer such exhortations, but there is very little they can do about it as a part of the professional process. (Beck, 1965, p. 6; quoted in Kadushin, 1965, p. 43)

Social Work Administration

The theory and practice of administration in the field of social work, which has received very little attention in the curriculum, is mentioned only in passing in the early issues of the *Journal*. "One area where there is now greater interest—but where progress has been slow indeed—is in developing in the master's program basic understanding of administration" (Stein, 1965, p. 65).

Student Discontent

While social work persists in its "tendency to see the social work curriculum content in terms that were truer twenty-five years ago than today," results of surveys conducted among students at two well-established and highly regarded schools of social work (Columbia University, 1960, and the University of Chicago, 1963) indicate the need to raise intellectual standards throughout the curriculum. "One might assume, with some warrant, that their statements about their programs are applicable to many other schools of social work" (Kadushin, 1965, p. 33).

Student complaints centered on the low level of academic content, the lack of challenge to intelligent students, and the greater emphasis on "feeling" than on "thinking." "On occasion, the most able students have shown similar dissatisfaction, and a number of the best students have withdrawn from the School, and from social work, in their disappointment" (p. 34).

Suggested reforms include "a more critical look" at needless repetition, frequently "substantial" in amount, and attention to "heavy, elaborate discussion of inconsequential trivia." The profession also should assume "more readiness to risk the students' exposure to divergent points of view" (p. 39).

Putting It Together

In summary, then, by 1965, the social work profession admits to a lack of theoretical underpinnings, unvalidated methods, a vague value system, a lack of research skills and potential, slow progress in the area of administration, student disenchantment, and a loss of social work's traditional clientele—the poor.

Flowing from these most basic problems are a host of others, not all of which will be enumerated here. These ongoing problems include sociological and psychological tensions, severe manpower shortages in general, and acute problems in staffing public assistance agencies in particular.

In 1963, Wilbur J. Cohen, Under Secretary of the Department of Health, Education, and Welfare, recognizing the seriousness of the social work manpower shortage, created a task force to estimate future needs and recommend measures for meeting them. The task force found that the number of qualified social work personnel in the United States was so low as to impair continuation of vital services as well as implementation of many new Congressional programs. Only 25% of the more than 125,000 persons engaged in providing social services in 1963–1964 had been trained in graduate schools of social work, and more than 12,000 vacancies for qualified personnel remained unfilled. The task force concluded that the shortage was destined to grow worse unless drastic measures were taken (Schottland, 1966, pp. 71, 73).

Still other problems are those of determining faculty requirements; problems relating to the doctoral program; problems relating to the effective, or not so effective, use of volunteers; and problems of validation of field work apprenticeship.

Having discovered that social work not only has alienated its traditional client, the poor, but is alienating many of its students, who presumably will minister to the poor, the reader of social work literature may be prepared to discover that one of the most far-reaching and decisive American social movements of recent years appears to have been alien to social work interests: "If one were to review the civil rights movement in the light of existing textbooks dealing with community organization—the closest thing we have to a social change method—one would conclude that the whole method of inducing social change that underlies the civil rights struggle is alien to social work" (Beck, 1965, p. 7).

MYSTERY: THE SECOND OPTION

Neither the problems of change nor professional self-doubts are the real causes for concern in estimating social work's view of itself 100 years after its founders decided to make charity scientific. Of genuine concern, however, are the level of development of the only institutionalized helping profession of broad public scope, the profession's own self-concept of its stage of development, and the steps being taken to move into adult professional status.

It may well be, as Younghusband contends, that professional social work still is in its infancy, although it has taken several centuries to bring it into existence. Or, as Pumphrey and Pumphrey (1961) have suggested, social work may need to be "helped out of its adolescence into a maturity which builds upon, rather than rejects, its history" (p. vi). Certainly, if the *Journal*, in marking social work's coming of age in 1965, feels "an inner urge to deepen knowledge and add to competence in teaching and practice . . . the mark of every true profession," students of that profession, as well as clients who rely on professional expertise, might well ask for more than a desire to know.

Abraham Flexner posed the obvious question as early as 1915. A medical educator, whose 1910 findings on the 155 medical schools in the United States and Canada resulted in large-scale reforms, Flexner turned his attention to social work. He began by asking: "Is Social Work a Profession?"

Pointing to the specialized and definite ends of such professions as architecture, medicine, and law, Flexner suggested: "Would it not be at least suggestive therefore to view social work as in touch with many professions rather than as a profession in and by itself?"

> To the extent that the social worker mediates the intervention of the particular agent or agency best fitted to deal with the specific emergency which he has encountered, is the social worker himself a professional or is he the intelligence that brings this or that profession or other activity into action? The responsibility for specific action thus rests upon the power he has invoked. The very variety of the situations he encounters compels him to be not a professional agent so much as the mediator invoking this or that professional agency. (Flexner, 1915, pp. 585–586)

These views met with less success than had Flexner's earlier criticisms of medical schools. His simple observations unwittingly helped to swing social work into psychiatric methods, to prove Flexner wrong and to justify its self-conscious professional identity (Bruno, 1957, p. 141; Klein, 1968, pp. 231–234). This wholesale adoption of the methods and insights of Freud, the Victorian Viennese, constituted social work's second major historical option.

With the advent of psychiatric concepts into social work, the historical door was closed firmly on the old C.O.S. volunteer image. In Younghusband's words, it was now demanded of the social worker

> "that she shall seek to understand the person in need, not only at that particular moment in time, but also the pattern of personality, the major experiences and relationships which make him the person he now is: with conflicts of whose origin he may be unaware; with problems whose solution may lie less in external circumstances than in his own attitudes, with tensions, faulty relationships, inabilities to face reality, hardened into forms he cannot alter without help. Instead of seeing his situation through her own eyes and producing already-made solutions, the social worker must be able to understand him and his needs and his relationships, as these appear to the person in need himself. She must enter into his problems as he sees them, his relationships as he experiences them, with their frustrations, their deprivations, their satisfactions, and see him, or his different selves, as they appear to him himself. Yet at the same time she must also be clearly aware of the realities of the situation and through her professional skill in relationships enable him to come to a better understanding of himself and others." (quoted in Morris, 1955, p. 199; in Wootton, 1959, p. 273)

Says Wootton: "It might well be thought that the social worker's best, indeed, perhaps her only, chance of achieving aims at once so intimate and so ambitious would be to marry her client" (p. 273).

Wooton notes, however, that Younghusband puts her faith in learning a body of knowledge and acquiring skills and wisdom which mellow through years of professional practice. It is this triadic acquisition which distinguishes the trained caseworker "from the 'good, sensible woman (or still more, man) with an all-around experience of life, who has travelled about the world a bit,' and who is widely, though not in her view wisely, believed to be 'just as, if not more valuable, than the specialized social worker' " (p. 273).

Thus was a profession born!

Freudian Deluge

Social work wholeheartedly embraced Freudianism, beginning in the years of the First World War and immediately after (Woodroofe, 1962, pp. 118–147). "At that time the American social work scene—

and a decade later the English scene—were swept by a psychiatric deluge which, for the time being at least, deflected thinking about social work into entirely new channels" (p. 119).

The National Conference of Social Work was swept up into the deluge in 1919. In her presidential address to the American Association of Psychiatric Social Workers 11 years later, Mildred Scoville spoke of the " 'realization in the social work field that all social case work has a psychological or mental hygiene aspect.' By 1940 . . . any deviation from 'Freudian psychology' in the theory of social work 'was looked upon by some with the same horror as a true Stalinist appraising a Trotskyite' " (Wootton, 1959, p. 270). "In a very few years practically the whole profession has succeeded in exchanging the garments of charity for a uniform borrowed from the practitioners of psychological medicine" (p. 270).

Kadushin (1959) complains that "the exclusiveness of the tie to psychoanalytic psychology is overstated" (p. 58). Yet his discussion of "The Rediscovery of the Social Sciences" and the institutionalization of psychoanalytic theory in organizational apparatus, the literature, and education, such that "no further explanation is needed to account for continuation," belies his own claim. At the same time, he quotes Eaton's observation that " 'until recently training in general personality theory [in schools of social work] was largely restricted to psychoanalysis" (p. 58; Eaton, 1956, p. 15).

As a matter of record, not only Wootton, but other authors more acceptable to the social work establishment, have provided hard evidence that social work seized upon psychoanalysis as a means of achieving professional status (Wootton, 1959, p. 270; Bruno, 1957, p. 141).

Like Bertram Beck, Kadushin sees social work as responding, in its incorporation of psychoanalysis, to the prevailing American spirit—a spirit which, following a period of great enthusiasm for social reform from 1890 to 1915, took a sharp turn in the 1920s. "At this time a psychological approach to the problem of the client was more relevant, more culturally pertinent, than the earlier sociological orientation" (Kadushin, 1959, p. 56).

> One might note that the emphasis on a treatment methodology as against a reform orientation made professionalization possible. We lacked then, and lack today, any adequate scientific base that would make possible professionalization of a social action approach. Psychoanalytic psychology, in offering a scientific base for the professionalization of methods of helping, encouraged the possibility of professionalization, which in turn strengthened this orientation. (p. 56, n. 27)

In short, there is strong justification for concluding that the major technical hallmark of the caseworker is the technique of relationship therapy. "This is a set of procedures of infinite variety, comprising almost entirely psychological concepts built upon psychoanalytic foundations. It is par excellence the casework technique as professed and taught today" (Klein, 1968, p. 165).

The literature on casework is vast. "No part of the field of social work has produced a comparable plethora of published material in books, periodicals, and conference reports. No part of the training program of social work schools has a comparable number of courses or as many course units, syllabi, or credit points. In addition, a very large number of case records used by many teachers of casework might be regarded as part—though unpublished—of the technique materials of the field." The methodology was largely, though not exclusively, psychoanalytical. "Casework had become relationship therapy within the psychoanalytic field of conceptual structure. There had to be retained, naturally, some recognition of nonpsychic factors, and there was also an attempt to establish rapport with sociological thinking" (Klein, 1968, p. 167).

Social work's recurring protestations of deep concern with the social, and its directives to bring the social back into social work, deserve more complete analysis at a later point. For now, it should be emphasized that social work's self-consciousness about its professional identity made it fearful of identification with the lowly status of social reform, while at the same time preventing it from borrowing the whole of psychology's resources.

> Does the competition with psychology for acceptance by psychiatry lead us to minimize the potential contribution of clinical psychology to our knowledge base? ... Would borrowing from the clinical psychologists emphasize our identification with them and consequently make more difficult the efforts at differentiation? ... Do we hesitate to turn to psychology for additions or amendments to such knowledge because this might be regarded as a betrayal of, or disloyalty to, psychiatry, a betrayal and disloyalty not involved in borrowing from sociology and anthropology? Are we threatened by valid divergencies between knowledge about process borrowed from psychiatry, which we have already incorporated, and what we might learn from psychology? Do we regard psychology as a Johnny-come-lately to the clinical setting and so tend to an *a priori* derogation of any contribution it might make to our knowledge base? (Kadushin, 1959, p. 73)

This shift by social workers to an almost exclusive dependence on psychoanalytic psychology reinforced the notion that casework is social work. Paradoxically, it also reinforced social work's historic, if unconscious, loyalties to Loch. Not only were clients seen merely as economically deserving or undeserving. By the 1920s, they also were seen as worthy of help only insofar as they were willing to be perceived not only as clients but as patients, subject to social work's quasi-scientific and quasi-medical ministrations. (Both scientific preoccupation and emphasis on knowledge of medicine, it should be noted, were to lose ground in succeeding years.)

Regardless of the presenting problems of the client—and very often they were the same as their deeper problems, namely, the effects of poverty—it now had become the social worker's mission to help the client uncover the forces by which he was being victimized—his unconscious drives, motivations, fixations. Social work had found its scientific justification in a new trinity of oral, anal, and genital in place of the old casework, group work, and community organization—or, rather, the new trinity was in some way to assimilate the old methods. Updated by Freud, social work now saw its mission, as did Loch, as " 'the work of the social physician' " (Woodroofe, 1962, p. 53).

Whatever one's views on the merits of Freud, or on critics such as Hans Eysenck (1966), social work's second major historical option in the first quarter of the 20th century was doomed to become obsolete. Given the haphazard nature of the social worker's training, Freudianism at its best, as interpreted by social workers, could be little more than a "bowdlerized version of psychoanalytic psychology, a sort of poor man's Freudianism that serves to legitimate the social worker's claim to help people in a 'scientific' way" (Berger, 1963, p. 4).

At its best, the new approach to helping embroiled both the social worker and the client in a new 20th-century straitjacket that was to prove as ineffectual in dealing with poverty as had been the C.O.S. method. At its worst, the new method was to become a type of witchcraft without license, often practiced harshly and intolerantly, not only on the client, but on students and faculty of schools of social work.

As late as the 1950s and 1960s, when social work already had declared itself on a new course of putting the social back into social work, there was too much Freudian emphasis in traditional treatment programs to allow client or student to conclude that Freudian pathways, now grown comfortable, might be rejected as sometimes ineffective, ludicrous, or dangerous.

Everyone who has had contact with social workers has favorite social work stories. One of mine has to do with a field worker who sent a social work school advisee of mine to look for a castration complex in a 9-year-old asthmatic in a federal housing project, nationally acknowledged as one of the federal government's prime high-rise errors.

The case of Sandra also comes to mind as an example of professional "listening with the third ear." As Sandra was being returned for the second time to the state school for delinquents, screaming and biting, the junior psychiatrist who was her social worker viewed the scene with equanimity. When two guards finally came to drag Sandra off, surreptitiously letting her scrape the pavement on the way, the social worker solemnly diagnosed: "Sandra really is saying that she is happy to be back with us."

Without denying the possibility that adolescents, like adults, often behave in ways alien to their true feelings, social work would benefit by starting with the known. There is the possibility of concluding that, given adequate cultural choices, adolescents would not prefer being confined in state schools to being left to their own devices on the outside.

These are relatively droll stories. Other experiences provided by psychoanalytically oriented social work are not amusing at all. As an educator who has seen students paraded into psychoanalysis, with the consequent stigma entered on records that went from agency to agency to be further reinterpreted by junior psychiatrists, it has always been a mystery to me why students did not select this particular violation of civil rights as the first object of student protest in its heyday.

As with clients generally, there is no reason to conclude that, when social work students disagree with faculty interpretations of life or Freud, gripe about programs or work loads, or express anxieties about personal identity or vocational choice, they are exhibiting a special category of pathological symptomology different from student reaction elsewhere. The choice of a life of service entails sufficient challenge to balanced functioning without the ever-present hazard of having dissension labeled as "needing psychiatric help" on student records by ill-equipped diagnosticians, not immune to idiosyncracies and neuroses of their own.

As a teacher and adviser, I have seen this happen more than a few times to students. Even on occasion when psychiatrists later called in for diagnosis were not in unanimous agreement with the social work diagnosis, the original record sometimes remained unchanged.

Need for Group Insights

If social workers claim that their present ineffectiveness stems from conceiving the individual too narrowly—at most, as an individual in a family—then, by hindsight, there was no other logical way of correcting the early influence of the C.O.S. than to move in the direction of those sciences which speak of the social group. Unfortunately, social work's choice, instead, was a wholesale, indiscriminate incorporation of psychoanalytic concepts. From this incorporation social work has never recovered.

Two views of the value of psychoanalytic theory for social work emerge in the literature.

Woodroofe (1962) sees the deluge of Freudianism as having left behind "rich alluvial soil in which new concepts were to take root and flourish, and older ones were to be vitalized and shaped anew" (pp. 119–120). This generally is the official position, though "some distortions in professional perception and activity" also may be noted as a consequence. *The Social Work Yearbook* for 1960 concludes that, since the 1920s, psychoanalytically oriented casework has contributed most of casework's understanding, with a small sector of caseworkers largely shaping casework's theory and practice. Secondary changes have continued to occur, reflecting changes and developments in psychoanalytic theory (Perlman, 1960, p. 537).

Wootton (1959) comments that these changes in favor of psychiatry, and especially psychoanalysis, have been welcomed with uncritical admiration. Admittedly, they have brought certain benefits. "They have . . . provided a way of escape from the inquisitorial methods by which the charitably disposed well-to-do persons previously sought protection, both for themselves against fraud, and for the community." At the same time, there has been a "great improvement in the standard of manners and courtesy which social workers think it proper to observe in their dealings with those whom they now call their 'clients.'" The price of these advantages, however, "has been the erection of a fantastically pretentious facade, and a tendency to emphasize certain aspects of social work out of all proportion to their real significance, while playing down others that are potentially at least as valuable. Nor is it certain that the substance of what social workers do to-day differs quite as radically as does the form from the parallels of an earlier epoch" (p. 271).

The growth of psychiatry and psychoanalysis came at a time when social workers were threatened with loss of employment, following the emergence of public relief services during the 1930s, as a response to the Great Depression. Deprived of their major function, and with subsidies from tax funds discontinued, voluntary casework agencies turned to casework services that could be developed independently of relief giving (Wootton, 1959, pp. 269–270). Psychiatry "provided social workers with just that new interpretation of their function of which they thus found themselves so badly in need" (p. 270).

The principle of individualization, "enunciated for the first time in 1886 [at the 13th National Conference of Charities and Correction] and still the foundation of modern casework" (Woodroofe, 1962, p. 120), thus was adapted to meeting the needs of the maladjusted, rather than the poor.

What of the Poor?

Wootton (1959) questions whether social work's predominant concern still is not with lower income groups, even if direct relief giving occupies less of the average social worker's activities than formerly. In 1950, she notes, 41% of all social workers in the United States were said to be employed in public assistance.

Whatever the facts, she concludes, it certainly is true that social workers do not see themselves primarily as dispensers of charity. Nor are they chiefly interested in the poverty of the poor. "Believing themselves, rightly or wrongly, to have been deprived of one function, they have lost no time in inventing another" (p. 270).

Social work began its new task of dispensing psychiatrically oriented casework by constructing modern definitions whose authors "seemed determined to outbid one another in the immensity of their claims." If taken at their face value, says Wootton, these modern definitions of casework "involve claims to powers which verge upon omniscience and omnipotence: one can only suppose that those who perpetuate these claims in cold print must, for some as yet unexplained reason, have been totally deserted by their sense of humour" (p. 271).

By 1949, Wootton reports, Swithun Bowers had found over 30 such definitions. He himself produced still another. Wootton sees the "most staggering" of American claims in Margaret Rich's statement to the Third International Conference of Social Work in 1936 (p. 272), in which she defined the "essential elements of the social case work process" to include

> (a) an attempt to understand the individual as a "psychobiological organism the functioning of which is determined by its structure and the peculiar development compelled by the interacting stimuli of inner needs and of environmental conditions and demands"; (b) sharing this understanding with the individual to the degree that he can accept and use it for further understanding of his difficulties and possibilities as a basis for developing his capacity to make his own social adjustment; (c) gauging the ability and tempo of the individual so as to free him from responsibilities too heavy for him to carry and at the same time to leave him to make use of available resources—educational, medical, religious, industrial—in working out his own social programs; (d) establishing a relationship with the individual through a willingness to let him "find himself without dictation, condemnation or didactic advice," thus making it possible for him "to work out an individual adjustment consonant with his own essential feelings and founded on his increased ability to utilize his personal and environmental resources." (Rich, 1938, pp. 476–477)

"After all this," concludes Wootton (1959), "it is not perhaps surprising to be told that the social caseworker who aims so high must be equipped with 'a definite body of knowledge about human behaviour, social relationships, social resources, and with the skills required to relate this knowledge to the individual situation.' He—or more probably she—will need them" (p. 272).

In England and Elsewhere

Both Wootton and Woodroofe agree that the psychiatric influx in England never reached the majestic swell of its American counterpart. For Woodroofe, what was a psychiatric deluge in America was a mere "trickle" in England in 1920, although it was to grow. According to Wootton (1959), "the [British] social workers' surrender to Freud has been less unquestioning." However, the influence of psychiatry was sufficient "to revolutionize both the language which these workers used and the conception of their role which they present alike to themselves and to others" (p. 270).

Several reasons are suggested for English resistance to Freud. "Perhaps the main reason was that the English social soil, fertilized as it was by the practice of Shaftesbury no less than the concepts of Owen, was not as receptive to individualist seeds as that of the New World" (Woodroofe, 1962, p. 139).

The foundation of the present English welfare state was laid, in the years from 1906 to 1912, as a result of the pressure to deal with poverty in a new way. By the beginning of the 20th century, the principle of "less eligibility" of the Act of 1834 was giving way to a newer concept of social welfare. These reforms were stimulated by those people who were not social work's forebears: Booth, B. Seebohm Rowntree, and the Fabian Society, vociferous critic of the existing order and archenemy of the C.O.S.

Despite these differences, the literature of England as well as America saw the injection of such medical terms as "diagnosis," "therapy," and "treatment" by the new social doctors, ranging from Mary E. Richmond's famous *Social Diagnosis* (1917) through Gordon Hamilton's 1940 *Theory and Practice of Social Case Work* (2nd ed., 1951), to Florence Hollis's *Casework: A Psychosocial Therapy* (1964).

England's classic statements in the psychiatric manner came from Eileen Younghusband. The European continent was similarly afflicted with casework overstatement, examples of which could be found as far north as Norway and as far south as Yugoslavia.

It is tempting to elaborate on the intricate and quite indistinguishable subtleties in the magic of the social worker's relationship with the client, "on the disciplined use of the worker's professional self"—a subject which receives a disproportionate share of attention in the Master's degree curriculum. It is this area that has given rise to the *Thousand Clowns* image.

The value of the professional relationship—not only for social workers, but for teachers, doctors, dentists, or storekeepers—does not have to be denied in order to reject the notion that social workers as a group have a special monopoly on the thing called "relationship." Despite the disproportionate amount of time spent by social workers in discussing this relationship, the professional image too often indicates just the opposite of the desired goal: the social work relationship often is stilted, lacking in warmth and in a perceptive sense of reality. Overconcentration on method does not make for humanly convincing problem solving.

At their most extreme, "descriptions of social work reach an almost mystical level" in the writings of Anita Faatz (Wootton, 1959,

p. 274). According to Faatz, in seeking help at a social work agency with such simple, practical problems as finding a job or a place to live, completing naturalization papers, or locating a doctor, " 'the concrete reality of the helping situation carries the true projection of the deepest conflict of the self,' so that 'help upon a practical, tangible life problem affords the potentiality for help which touches the core of the self and sets in motion an authentic process of growth;' and 'out of a helping process there eventuates, in slow growth, an experience in which there is a heightened sense of life; as if here, in this moment of time, has been manifest an expression of movement and change like a veritable piece of life itself' " (Wootton, 1959, pp. 274–275; Faatz, 1953, pp. 43, 65).

Even the simple mechanics of spacing the interview sessions are touched by the near-mysticism of involvement: " 'When interviews are spaced at weekly intervals, as they very frequently are in the casework service, the hour of engagement between the helper and the one who seeks help can be intense, deeply disturbing, and penetrated by the new sense of life which every human being fears intensely yet craves so deeply. A week is none too long in which to thrash about in one's own aloneness—in confusion, in rebellion, in yielding, in conflict, all gathering toward the moment of return, in new organization, in new discovery of what the self is like by telling it to another whose responses are accurate' " (Wootton, 1959, p. 275; Faatz, 1953, pp. 134–135).

The Case of Jane

Wootton's comments on relationship are some of the most delightful in social work literature, and while social workers of the 1960s were fond of saying that Wootton already was "old hat"—meaning the profession had advanced far beyond her criticism—students still plowed through Casework I, II, III, and sometimes "Advanced," with the old psychiatric guidelines.

The case of Jane kept being repeated, with variations on the theme. Jane, brought to a Midwestern state school for delinquency because of chronic promiscuity, was given an impressive psychiatric diagnosis that suggested "lack of ego strength." The staff helped build up Jane's ego by a program of weight watching, hair, makeup, and dress correction, and psychiatrically tinged therapy in which a therapist listened to Jane's dreams, propitiously taking place in full color. This close, one-to-one relationship progressed to increasingly glowing reports of strengthened ego control, with only one skeptical soul remaining, the ground workman, who was heard to observe that someone should listen to Jane as she washed windows. When Jane's ego strength had been built up sufficiently, she was given an extended weekend holiday as reward, at which time she took off with five boys on motorcycles—a numerical increase over the original problem.

Clients and the public might well appreciate an increase in competence and reality therapy and a decrease in relationship.

Thus did the friendly visitor of the Old Charity Organisation Society of 1883, investigating the suitability of granting a small sum of money to a client who wished to begin life as a hawker of table brushes, take on modern garb. In 1948, a social worker of the Family Service Association of America, called upon to help an unhappy client with a problem of "unsatisfactory job adjustment," painstakingly pursued "inner problems, tensions and fears" with the help of intelligence, aptitude, and Rorschach tests, and examination at intervals by a psychiatrist. The diagnosis included: "Emotionally still in need, like the child, of looking to adults for security, reassurance of his strength, and help in controlling his impulses." Woodroofe (1962) comments that the task of helping this unhappy client, with adult responsibilities of marriage and parenthood, to overcome his handicap of emotional immaturity and reach an understanding of himself obviously was considered more beneficial than giving him sufficient financial backing to enable him to seek another job (pp. 118–119).

Though one may credit this new approach with an improvement in manners toward the client, the tool of psychiatry has the potential of becoming a dangerous authoritarian weapon in unskilled hands—and, some believe, in skilled hands as well. When clients are seen as emotionally in need of authority figures to uncover the causes of their malfunctioning, they then become children to be diagnosed by social work students. These students, in turn, become children to be diagnosed by older holders of the M.S.W., who are now administrators and teachers, while newly or differently trained faculty and other miscreants become a special sort of children, to be analyzed in the pecking order of existing authority.

Social workers rarely make clear distinctions between their work as a technology or an art, which as art should have all the fluidity and grace consonant with the unexplored complexity of the human condition. Consequently, one of the results of the psychiatric deluge was the acquisition of a method that gave social work a new intolerance and authoritarianism. An art form was advanced to the level of dogma.

MAGIC: THE THIRD OPTION

Flexner did not succeed in dissuading social work from thinking of itself as a profession. On the contrary, his comments of 1915 served to spur the third major historical option of the helping art: the achievement of professional status as a primary aim.

In this single-minded pursuit, the cost, magic talk, was not seen as too high. As with many public relations efforts, legitimate aspiration became an imagined reality, making mischief in curriculum offerings and theoretical attempts.

What social work said and thought of itself, however—its claim to a type of universal understanding denied to older professions, which were limited to only one facet of client life, while social work had the gestalt of the generic (Lurie, 1954, p. 36)—was not similarly appreciated by other professions. The Carr-Saunders and Wilson (1933) comprehensive study of the professions did not include social work, nor did it explain the omission. Since 1925, of at least 25 studies published in the United States and abroad on occupational prestige, only a few have included social work as one of the occupations selected for examination (Kadushin, 1958, p. 40).

As late as 1968, it was not felt necessary to explain the omission of social work from the Carr-Saunders and Wilson study. Herman D. Stein, writing on "Professions and Universities" (1968), stated: "Any discussion of professions instantly requires paying respects to the pioneer work of Carr-Saunders and Wilson, on the history of the professions in England particularly, and on the European continent and the developing countries generally" (p. 53). With that out of the way, Stein decides not to discuss his profession at all, either from the Carr-Saunders and Wilson viewpoint or any other. "I will not dwell on my own profession, social work—which I dare to call a profession" (p. 58).

Wootton and Klein are both inclined to disagree with Stein on this last point. "Actually, the pretense that professional casework is of a piece with other more established professions can only be maintained by disregarding some very obvious differences" (Wootton, 1959, p. 287). "If Dr. Abraham Flexner were now to discuss whether social work is a profession, in the light of his standards, he would hesitate less than ever to come to the conclusion that it had missed the boat, and is slowly, though loudly, paddling backward" (Klein, 1968, p. 218).

Ernest Greenwood, in "Attributes of a Profession" (1957), observes: "The preoccupation of social workers with professionalization has been a characteristic feature of the social work scene for years. Flexner, Johnson, Hollis and Taylor, and others have written on the subject, proposing criteria which must be met if social work is to acquire professional status. Whenever social workers convene, there is the constant reaffirmation of the urgency to achieve the recognition from the community befitting a profession" (p. 54).

Greenwood himself makes the claim that "social work is already a profession; it has too many points of congruence with the model to be classifiable otherwise" (p. 54). His model, built "after a careful canvass of the sociological literature on occupation," has five distinguishing elements: (1) systematic theory, (2) authority, (3) community sanction, (4) ethical codes, and (5) a culture.

William E. Gordon, who in 1965 was suggesting not a contribution to the body of systematic theory necessary for professional status, but merely a tentative working frame of reference for such a theory, calls the Greenwood discussion a "scholarly article." Gordon himself says flatly: "Since social work is a profession, a proposed frame of reference must also be consistent with the notion of the profession and its role" (p. 22).

Whether social work should seek professionalization on the grounds that "the prestige of the profession affects the effectiveness with which the worker offers a service" (Kadushin, 1958, p. 37) is a separate question, in view of social work's past and present limitations in meeting client needs.

The fact is, as the literature of social work clearly demonstrates, that the preoccupation of social workers with professionalization has been a characteristic feature of the social work scene for years. The more immediate question is what this guilt-ridden, compulsive search has contributed to the product social workers offer and to the process by which they acculturate their students and clientele.

There is no question that confusion reigns among social workers about the exact level of professionalization of their work. Whereas Klein suggests that Flexner would be disappointed in social work's present-day achievement, Henry J. Meyer (1959) arrives at precisely the opposite conclusion: "Any discussion of social work as a profession in the United States today must face a number of ambiguities. . . . There need be no ambiguity, however, about the old question put to social work by Abraham Flexner in 1915: Is social work a profession? The professional status of social work is generally acknowledged" (p. 319).

What might be dismissed as a problem of semantics takes on new weight when one considers the arbitrariness and authoritarianism that too frequently attach themselves to social work notions of the professional relationship. Greenwood (1957) writes:

> In a professional relationship . . . , the professional dictates what is good or evil for the client, who has no choice but to accede to professional judgment. Here the premise is that because he lacks the requisite theoretical background, the client cannot diagnose his own needs or discriminate among the range of possibilities for meeting them. Nor is the client considered able to evaluate the caliber of the professional service he receives. In a nonprofessional occupation the customer can criticize the quality of the commodity he has purchased, and even demand a refund. The client lacks this same prerogative, having surrendered it to a professional authority. (p. 48)

If purchasers of professional services were ever so docile and unthinking, the present mood of clients, disadvantaged and otherwise, makes this claim for social work authority fatuous. "One thing is certain," Klein (1968) concludes. "Until the extent and nature of client needs become the proper focus of planning, and the ambitions of professional personnel take their appropriate place as auxiliary motivations, the development of effective welfare programs will come increasingly from the leadership of economic and political thinkers in government, universities, and the press" (p. 294). And, it should be added, from indigenous client thrust.

The Generic: Comedy of the Absurd

What is the pathway by which social work has or has not become a profession? How successful has been the search for the generic, which, simply stated, is an effort to find the common underpinnings of all social work ministration?

In brief, social work has continued to employ the concept of the generic, even without specific content, and despite growing confusion, for two reasons: (1) the hope of establishing methodological conciseness; and (2) the hope of "scientizing" social work's function into professional respectability.

Although the term *generic* has been "loosely employed without careful definition," notes Bartlett (1959), "since its appearance three decades ago, the generic-specific concept has dominated social work thinking. It has been valuable in moving the profession to its present stage."

> Educators have used it from one orientation and practitioners from another. Since the assumptions related to each of these orientations were not usually made explicit, educators and practitioners although using the same words, were frequently not communicating with each other. The thinking never progressed to the point where an authorita-

tive statement, acceptable and useful to the whole profession, was produced. A social work committee planning a research project could not find such a basic formulation in the literature, although many vigorous and stimulating statements were noted. (pp. 159–160)

By 1959, the generic-specific issue was seen as one of five central issues facing social work. Alfred J. Kahn, editor of *Issues in Social Work* (1959), gave a new start to the continuing search by defining social work's unique orientation "in its broad sense." He saw it as growing out of a value core and perspective characterized by "concern for person-in-the-situation, and group-in-community, community-in-society, or in short, an integrative view of the individual or the human situation. This rather than one methodological key is what is crucial" (p. 26).

Social work has developed no authoritative single statement of what is generic, and no comprehensive analysis of the generic-specific concept is available in the literature (Bartlett, 1959, p. 173). A historical sketch of the understanding or misunderstanding of the term must depend largely on two articles: Harriet M. Bartlett's "The Generic-Specific Concept in Social Work Education and Practice" (1959) and Katherine A. Kendall's "A Conceptual Framework for the Social Work Curriculum of Tomorrow" (1953). In addition, Ruth Elizabeth Smalley (1967) provides several pages on the pursuit of the generic, as it was related to the growth of professional social work organizations (pp. 5–15).

Milford Conference

The generic-specific concept is considered to have been set forth "clearly" for the first time in the Report of the Milford Conference, a voluntary committee of social workers who began meeting in 1923 because they felt that practice had outrun formulation and orderly analysis was needed. This first formal use of the generic-specific concept was concerned only with social casework.

Social work developed as a profession in no neat, logical way, explains Smalley. Programs of service arose haphazardly, in this country and elsewhere, to meet needs of individuals, groups with specific social problems, the homeless, handicapped children and adults, the mentally ill, and the poor.

The creation in 1878 of a Conference of Charities and Corrections, which separated itself at that time from the American Social Science Association, was an early attempt to identify a commonness or unity in what was, in many respects, a diversity of efforts. It was the Milford Conference which "made an historic contribution to the development of social work as a single profession through its identification of the 'generic' in social casework practice" (Smalley, 1967, p. 6).

With regard to the tendency to create specialized forms of social casework under different agency auspices, the Milford Report stated, " 'the outstanding fact is that the problem of social casework and the equipment of the social caseworkers are fundamentally the same for all fields.' " Generic social casework " 'was conceived as embodying such elements as: knowledge of norms and deviations of social life; methods of particularizing the human individual and using community resources in social treatment; the adaptation of scientific knowledge and formulations of experience to social casework; and a conscious philosophy' " (Bartlett, 1959, pp. 160–161).

Thus spoke the sponsors of the Milford Report, leaving to others the task of defining exactly what content was generic in social casework. The Report obviously embraced the notion that all practice of social casework rested on a single theory, philosophy, and method, as well as on certain undefined, but ultimately definable, scientific formulations of human experience.

It should be observed that, in announcing rather prematurely that there was such a thing as generic casework, the Milford Report was attempting to tidy up a professional occupation in much the same way as the Charity Organisation Society had attempted to tidy up haphazard methods of charity granting. Both aims, reasonably legitimate, were to force social workers into an overriding concern with method as opposed to content. The Freudian option, as interpreted by social workers, had much the same effect.

The final report of the Milford Committee in 1929, "Social Case Work, Generic and Specific," proposed something of a logical contradiction. It was to be only a beginning exploration of the generic, on the assumption that specific aspects of casework would be taught in classroom and field. Nevertheless, the Report stressed the central importance of generic social casework, which " 'means chiefly the adaptation of the various concepts, facts and methods which we have discussed as generic social casework to the requirements of the specific field' " (Bartlett, 1959, p. 161). Generic casework was to be the adaptation of undefined concepts, facts, and methods, called "generic" by the Milford group, to the requirements of specific fields, which were to be taught in the classroom and in field work.

Thus began the search for a magical entity that was declared to be present. Social workers were exhorted to adapt it to specific fields. Researchers were encouraged to find it and clarify it. The history of that search is, by its nature, an exposition of magic talk.

The early Milford invitation to ferret out the generic in social casework produced numerous responses, but many of these resulted only in a confounding of confusion (Kendall, 1953, p. 26). In the end, constant discussion about the generic promise, increasing after

World War Two, "reinforced the generic concept and gave the false impression that a common practice really existed and was understood. Thus the final outcome was a kind of fluid thinking about practice which had genuine vitality but was inconsistent and full of gaps because of the failure to come to grips with the problems involved in an orderly analysis of social work practice as a particular phenomenon" (Bartlett, 1959, p. 166).

It is interesting to speculate, says Bartlett, why the urgent request for research in social casework fell unheeded. Had such research been undertaken, "the extension of the concept from social casework to social work as a whole could have been more soundly carried through. Many of the present confusions would have been avoided. Finally, the imbalance between education and practice would not have occurred" (p. 166). As it was, an empty concept was extended to the whole of social work and used to judge curricular requirements through the years.

Grace F. Marcus (1938–39) "confirmed the thinking" in the Milford Report with the following statement, however nonclarifying:

> The term generic does not apply to any actual, concrete practice of an agency or field but refers to an essential common property of case work knowledge, ideas and skills which case workers of every field must command if they are to perform adequately their specific jobs. As for our other troublemaking word, "specific," it refers to the form case work takes within the particular administrative setting; it is the manifest use to which the generic store of knowledge has been put in meeting the particular purposes, problems, and conditions of the agency and in dispensing its particular resources. (pp. 3–4; quoted in Bartlett, 1959, p. 162)

By 1959, Bartlett herself was interested neither in a new definition nor in extensive analysis of the literature, but in identifying major phases and future directions. She felt that greater clarity would be achieved by viewing the generic-specific as "an inclusive concept, composed of two sub-concepts which are interdependent and complementary in meaning" (p. 159), although she defines neither subconcept.

In her treatment of the generic, Bartlett felt it appropriate to put the words "specialized" and "specialization" in quotation marks when used in ways she considered inaccurate or vague (p. 173). Consequently, "specialized" and "specialization" appear in quotation marks at least 20 times. "Specific" appears seven times. She concludes that "the most consistent stream of thinking regarding practice in the thirties and early forties was to be found in the studies being undertaken by the 'specialized' professional organizations" (pp. 166–167).

Group Work, Community Organization

At one time, group work and community organization were treated as specializations. With the application of the term *generic* to all of social work, confusion, as Bartlett notes, became pervasive. "Specific" and "specialized" were employed interchangeably; distinctions between specialization in practice and "expertness" in performance were not perceived; emphases and uses shifted over time.

As late as 1953, Kendall worried about a hypothetical case involving the profession's "approval of specializations within a specialization—a specialization which is, in fact, a generic method" (p. 26).

Kendall, who argues for further generic attempts, despite difficulty, admits that the profession must face frankly the fact that its classification of "specialized" and "generic" is unclear.

> In the light of our history of development, it is perhaps inevitable that group work . . . should go through a phase of high specialization before it becomes distinctive enough to be assimilated as a generic process. But how long must we continue to live with the inconsistency of our position? What are we to do, for example, if a school that offers group work rather than casework as the basic process applies for accreditation? The curriculum policy statement affirms that group work provides basic preparation for social work practice. Do we then accredit the school, thus accepting group work as generic, and then ask it to submit an application for approval to offer a group-work specialization? (p. 26)

Generic Organization

However elusive the generic concept was to prove itself, the very variety of programs of service in which social work had its origins affected future organization efforts. Historically, social workers were arranged both according to field of practice, such as psychiatric or medical social workers, and according to method of practice, such as social group work.

Even before the Milford Conference and the decision to call social casework "generic," the notion of underlying unity in diversity had entered social workers' minds. Smalley (1967) calls the American Association of Social Workers, organized in 1921, the first " 'generic' membership organization for all practicing social workers" (p. 7).

The organization included individuals unaffiliated with a social work organization, as well as social work membership organizations, each with its own requirements for membership and group functioning. What Smalley euphemistically calls a "generic" organization still retained as its chief function that of an employment agency. The parent organization was the National Social Workers Exchange, an employment agency dating from 1916 as the Department of Social Work of the Intercollegiate Bureau of Occupations.

From its beginnings, the Exchange had involved intellectual and administrative leaders of the new field of social work, as well as the pioneer philanthropic foundation established to advance the interests of social work, The Russell Sage Foundation. It devoted itself early to questions about the nature of the potential profession and the specialized training provided in schools of social work, seen as the profession's mark of distinction. Klein concludes that, even though employment in a social agency of "recognized standing" was a condition of professional standing, school training probably was the central moving concept (p. 204).

As the American Association of Social Workers, still concerned largely with employment, the new organization had a special service attraction to women who, coincidentally, were enjoying the first fruits of their hard-won franchise.

In a formal sense, says Klein (1968), the profession of social work came into existence in 1921–22, when the American Association of Social Workers was organized. In a less formal but perhaps more significant sense, the profession was born in 1898, when the Charity Organization Society of New York initiated its first brief training course, which soon came to be the New York School of Philanthropy. "The schools for training social workers were from the very beginning the spiritual soil on which the profession and early professional standards were built" (p. 203).

Calling the American Association of Social Workers a "generic" organization was undoubtedly premature, since it was only in 1955, with the creation of the National Association of Social Workers, "that the profession found a commonness in values, purposes, program, and practice methods sufficient to permit a single organization, requiring for membership a single educational base" (Smalley, 1967, p. 8).

That educational base was facilitated by the establishment three years earlier, in 1952, of the present Council on Social Work Education, which laid the foundation for central development of curricula and accreditation of schools of social work and made graduation from an accredited graduate School of Social Work a feasible requirement for membership in the NASW.

Even in 1955, however, the hope of the generic was not to be realized definitively in the NASW, as debates continued over organizational sections such as medical, psychiatric, school, social group, social research, and community organization. Not all members shared generic hopefulness, and there were differences of opinion as to the meaning of the term. Social work practice in special fields received continued support from such organizations as the Family

Service Association of America, The Child Welfare League, the American Public Welfare Association, the National Social Welfare Assembly, and various governmental agencies at federal, state, and local levels.

The initial period of organization of the American Association of Social Workers undeniably reinforced a commitment to social work as a new profession and to the ideals of democratic social reform. Leaders of the Association denounced child labor and espoused protection of women in industry, as well as broader labor legislation. Social workers offered testimony at Congressional hearings and later set up a lobbying and information office of the Association in Washington. *The Social Work Year Book* and the *Encyclopedia of the Social Sciences* were produced with Association cooperation. The Association undertook its own publications in the *Journal of Social Work*, monographs, and a newsletter (Klein, 1968, pp. 204–205).

What the new Association did not do—following in the tradition of its predecessors in the old Charity Organisation Society—was attempt any serious consideration of and attack on the basic problems of their clients. "What was never seriously undertaken was any responsibility for, or active leadership in, attacking poverty as a major pathology in the current civilization. Nor did it face the problems of destitution as constituting a primary obligation of the personnel of the Association, though it had been claiming special competence, skill, and historical continuity in the field" (Klein, 1968, pp. 205–206). The historic option of professionalization was no more productive of broad social reform than were the options of methodizing charity or curing clients by psychiatric method.

Social work, through its new organization, was not alone in failing to discern the structural causes of poverty and its related problems. As the 20th century progressed and new understandings emerged, however, the Association became more engrossed in concern for the first of its organizational goals: to protect the interests and status of the practitioner. In effect, this objective took precedence over its two other stated goals: to protect the persons or public to be served; and to advance the competence of the worker and his usefulness to general welfare.

Klein (1968) observes: "Since the personnel of the social services is by definition expected primarily to promote the public interest, it would follow that the first of the functions listed above would be least important, while the other two are sometimes indistinguishable from each other" (p. 202). Klein questions whether even the interests of the practitioner relating to security of tenure or appropriate compensation have been advanced effectively by the professional organization, since these goals have become chiefly the concern of labor unions in the field (p. 202, n. 3).

With the growth of NASW membership, the potential for social reform lessened, and the impetus of the early American Association pioneers was largely submerged in the following organizational characteristics:

Persons formally qualified for membership in the professional association are a minority of the persons engaged in welfare services.

A diminishing proportion is engaged in what was in the earlier period the settlement field with its active role in social reform and neighborhood service.

The casework membership has become a self-conscious elite, and within that group the psychiatric technique of casework has become predominant.

Interest in destitution and poverty has become less and less, and the influence of the group in that field has declined.

Activities on the organizational level of the association have veered toward advancing and preserving interests of the worker as against those of the client, in a manner often verging on a caste-like trend, and the worker is increasingly being defined as "member of the NASW." (Klein, 1968, p. 207)

Despite these obvious deficiencies in social commitment and perceptiveness, the search for the generic continued and still continues unabated. Professional exclusiveness is an echo of Beatrice Webb's (1926) observation that, instead of serving as a coordinating group to all the other charities, "the C.O.S. became itself the most exclusive of sects, making a merit of disapproving and denouncing much of the practice of other charitable agencies ... and at the same time failing to obtain anything like the army of personal 'friends of the poor,' or anything approaching the great amount of money, that would have enabled it to cope, on its own principles, with the vast ocean of poverty that had somehow to be dealt with" (p. 197).

FORWARD TO THE FOUNDING FATHERS: THE FIRST WISDOM

In the decade following World War Two, when, according to Bertram Beck, schools of social work were not able to meet social action goals nor attain a role in social policy which many leaders desired, the profession turned again to one of its "perennial" questions: the nature of and the means to achieving the "social" in social work.

In 1959, Beck observed "that the problem social work faces today as a profession concerned with affecting the nature of society and also dealing with the impact of society on groups, individuals, and communities is as old as the profession. Because of its persistency one may fairly conclude that the problem is inherent in social work's unique task" (p. 194).

Neither the advocates of "methods and techniques" nor the advocates of "social action," says Beck, deny social work's dual responsibility. Rather, the protagonists of these two positions—at first view, crucially differing positions—merely seek a proper balance and function. This balance must shift as the scientific base on which social work draws develops and as the society in which social work functions changes. "The examination of the problem is, therefore, a task which must be tackled anew by succeeding generations of social workers, not with a view to disentangling the necessary organic unity of cause and function in social work, but with a view to finding the appropriate balance and relationship for the particular generation" (pp. 194-195).

The notion that social work, despite historical fact to the contrary, always has recognized a changing organic unity of individual and society and has merely to translate that unity into appropriate contemporary emphasis is a distinct element of social work's educational *mystique*. The pursuit of the social in social work, like the pursuit of the relational principle and the pursuit of the generic, is bolstered by a magic talk that would seem to doom social work to a perpetual wish-world of discussion in which the social is more to be theoretically admired than emulated.

When the question of the social is raised periodically, its advocates find themselves generally agreeing with critics of social work that, if social work cannot influence the social policies that create social problems, it will dispense merely technical help, while ignoring the real infection. In time, social work will be occupied entirely with picking up the pieces of those who break under the burdens of modern society, and ultimately it will become an instrument that seeks adjustment above all else (Beck, 1959, p. 191).

Training for Social Work: Third International Survey (United Nations, 1958) admits that social workers are perhaps insufficiently aware of their obligation to translate their experience of the needs of individual clients into better social welfare provision. When social workers are far better grounded in psychology and sociology than at present, "and when they have more skill in working with groups as well as individuals, they should be in a position to make a major contribution as consultants on the social aspects of institutional care" (p. 66).

Social workers "are just barely beginning" to play their part in planning services and policies which might prevent the rise of social or personal ills, although, according to the *Survey*, the methods of casework, group work, and community organization, as well as rudimentary social research, were inherent in the work of the early leaders. We already have discussed the fiction that social work's immediate ancestors, beginning with the C.O.S., were interested in social structural problems of society, as well as the historic preeminence of casework among the methods of the profession.

Social work's hope, apparently, lies in recapturing an "early wisdom"—that pristine period when social work was at peace with the social sciences. "For some years now, social work education has been striving to recapture its lost early wisdom and to learn to apply, adapt and expand American methods and literature creatively in different social conditions and cultures" (United Nations, 1958, pp. 119–120). The way ahead lies, according to the *Survey* authors, in the alliance of sociology, psychiatry, social work, and administration.

And what of that early wisdom to which social work need only return—"returning to its origins, though on a higher level of the spiral, and with major advances in the behavioural and social sciences incorporated into its methodology" (United Nations, 1958, p. 107)?

Without a definitive history of social work, details of social work's rapprochement with the social sciences and social action must be pieced together. In summary, it seems clear that this early wisdom was of extremely short duration, both in England and in the United States, to be attained again only momentarily throughout social work's century of existence.

Social Work Was Casework

Walter Kindelsperger's 1966 observation is a succinct appraisal of the long-term situation that has given rise to the modern problem of the social in social work. Until recently, he says, it was not uncommon to hear the terms *casework* and *social work* used as synonyms for the same activity. "Gradually the concept of social worker expanded to include group work, community organization, and administration. This development came during the period of unification of practice under the generic banner. These changes were more or less parallel to the process that brought the professional association together" (p. 46).

Younghusband's report of the intercultural seminar of social workers held in 1966 offers some insight into the profession's present knowledge of group and community methods. The seminar devoted almost no discussion to group work, except for a brief reference to the value of group experience for the individual as a means of learning to function better socially. There was regret "that group work had progressed from recreational activities to group therapy without developing a wider range of methods and skills in working with a variety of normal groups, a development that might have provided some of the much-needed practice skills in various segments of work with communities" (p. 64).

On community work, the participants emphasized that such work normally is not concerned with pathology or deviance. They agreed that community work does not always operate in situations where there is consensus on the nature of a given social need or on aims and methods. The seminar suggested: "In conflict situations, the aim is to bring about resolution or compromise without open aggression or ostracism or withdrawal. No matter what the circumstances, the aim is always better allocation of resources, community cohesion, ability to identify and meet needs, and ability to cope with conflict without disruption" (p. 65).

Whatever the original wisdom, the fall was great indeed. Since group work and community organization were not included in the original wisdom, a return to better days must be sought elsewhere. In the 1960s, while American cities were set afire in civil protest, and news of the Third World revolution had reached even the nonprofessional, social workers of the world were seriously and professionally warned to guard against a hidden program agenda in community work; to avoid being drawn into taking sides with one group against another; to maintain clarity about processes at work in the community and social work aims in diffuse situations; and to take care not to relinquish their professional role in community activities, whereby they would become simply a "good sort" in that community (Younghusband, 1966, p. 65).

Who Are We?

The quest for a return to original wisdom is further complicated by two social work realities: the problem of self-identity and the more embracing problem of what is relevant for social work borrowing. Both problems are reflections of social work's previous historical choices against the social. Caught in the throes of an identity crisis, filled with further confusion about the nature of the relevant, social workers naturally react with pain and defensiveness.

There is no doubt about social work's present identity crisis. "Indecision and milling around on decisions related to change appears to be influenced by a lack of a conception or image of the social worker of the future. This confusion is accentuated in practice by what we are already doing" (Kindelsperger, 1966, p. 41). Central to the confusion are those "individuals conceiving of themselves as 'the social worker,' but experiencing great difficulty in developing an appropriate image to encompass the many facets of current practice. Part of our difficulty is a custom of neat and limited classification such as 'case workers' or 'group workers' " (p. 46).

Kadushin sees a deeper reason for the current problem of identity. Social work is concerned not only with the perennial problem of the individual versus the social, but with the more fundamental, also perennial, problem of what is relevant. He admits that, if relevance were the primary factor in determining the direction in which social work turned for help, casework, at least, would be developing a more active interchange with psychology, sans psychiatric overtones.

Relevance to our needs, he says, may not be the primary factor in determining borrowing simply because social work is not clear as to what is relevant. This is a perennial problem of social work and the fundamental problem in establishing a firm knowledge base. "In 1931 Karpf noted that it was necessary to answer the question of what is social work and who is a social worker 'if the processes and procedures of social work were to be analyzed for determining the type of knowledge on which they are based.' Yet the answer was not available then. Nor is it available today" (Kadushin, 1959, p. 75; Karpf, 1931, p. 2).

Both Kadushin and Beck recognize the present urgency of resolving the problems of identity, academic borrowing, and effective social action.

Beck estimated in 1959 that, although social work was not ready to discharge its social action function, it was "closer to readiness than at any other point in its history" (p. 213). In the same year, Kadushin hazarded: "Perhaps . . . there is basis for the hope that we are ready for an answer" (1959, p. 76).

Though social work's critics have attributed to social workers a

70

lack of interest in broad social policy—as did the Hollis and Taylor social work statement of 1951 (p. 141)—"there is little evidence to support the charge of lack of interest, and it seems probable that lack of effectiveness would be a more accurate allegation" (Beck, 1959, p. 201).

Beck insists that early social work leaders were in the vanguard of social reform, enlisting in their ranks those who fought such evils as destitution, ill health, and poor housing. He argues that if the founders of the social work profession had been content merely with doling out a pittance of relief, they could not have laid the foundation of a profession, with "its growing ability" to base practice on theory drawn from the biological, behavioral, and social sciences (p. 191).

Beck points to the proceedings of the National Conference on Social Welfare to demonstrate that there has been no lack of persons to call attention to the social reform function. "While concerns certainly shifted from the broad, idealistic, self-confident approach that marked early conferences, the *Proceedings* for practically every year are replete with accounts of solid gains made in terms of more adequate social provisions" (p. 201).

Beck also notes that, at the formation of the National Association of Social Workers in 1955—a fairly late date in social work history—one of the first acts of the Board of Directors was to rank social policy with social work practice as a top priority, reflected in the appointment of a legislative representative in Washington. By 1958, 78% of local chapters had committees on social work practice. "Available evidence, therefore, suggests that social workers do not need their interest in social policy stimulated but they do need help in translating that interest into action most effectively and in developing and maintaining an interest in perfecting their practice as keen as their interest in social action" (p. 202).

In Kadushin's view, the inadequacies of social work reflect, to a large extent, the inadequacies of the behavioral sciences generally. He sees justification for the old quip that social work is an art based on a science not yet invented (1959, p. 77, n. 82). Kadushin concludes, however, that the need for a firm knowledge base is more urgent now than it was 30 years ago:

> The necessity to prove ourselves to a patient society is greater now. The failings of childhood are not excusable in the young adult. Are the consequences of intercession by the trained social worker in the life of the client—individual, group, or community—significantly different from the results achieved by the layman or untrained worker? Maybe this is so and we cannot effectively prove it. However, the evidence which is available is equivocal. Our inability clearly to answer in the affirmative is partly a result of our inadequate knowledge base. (p. 77)

Critical Views

Critics of social work are much less sanguine in their assessments. Two former Secretaries of Health, Education, and Welfare have addressed themselves to the problem of social work effectiveness.

In 1962, Abraham Ribicoff complained that social workers have been inconspicuous for too long around the committee rooms, state legislatures, and halls of Congress. "It does not matter—for purposes of my argument here—whether you are employed in public welfare or in voluntary organization. Your budgets and the extent, emphasis, and effectiveness of your work are all dependent on political processes and the climate of public opinion" (p. 3).

Ribicoff challenged the profession to take an active part in shaping laws and public policies, observing that "you have not wielded your influence to anywhere near the degree your unique fund of knowledge and your skill of working with people might warrant." He pointed to the need for constructive change in the entire field of social welfare. "An unsentimental, informed social work voice is urgently needed as we in public welfare set out on a significant reorientation of our basic programs which were established through the Social Security Act more than a quarter-century ago" (p. 3).

In 1966, another former Secretary of Health, Education, and Welfare challenged social workers with a picture of the social work school of 1990. John W. Gardner predicted that the lineal descendants of present social work educators will tell students that, sometime in the late 1960s, the profession decided it was self-defeating to build walls between itself and its natural allies—fellow professionals, subprofessionals, technicians, and semi-skilled workers. Future educators also will recall that social work leaders in the late 1960s decided they not only must continue to strengthen the master's and doctoral programs, but also must accept roles of leadership in educational programs at the two-year and four-year college level, and even at the high school level (pp. 7–8).

Gardner warned that schools and professions are subject to the same deadening forces that afflict other human institutions: "an attachment to time-honored ways, reverence for established procedures, a preoccupation with one's own vested interests, and an excessively narrow definition of what is relevant and important" (p. 7).

"The peaks lie ahead of you—but whether you scale them depends on your own vision and boldness" (p. 9).

The Peak of 1903

If we are to take social work literature seriously, social work's first peak occurred in 1903, the year in which the School of Sociology of the Charity Organisation Society in England was founded. "How promising and how full of vigour was social work in England fifty years ago!" exclaimed Younghusband in 1953. This is the ideal to which modern social work must somehow return, the period of early wisdom (Younghusband, 1964, pp. 15–22).

We already have discussed social work's historical optimism in including pioneers such as Booth in its ancestral tree; in seeing methods such as group work and community organization as "inherent in the work of the early leaders" (United Nations, 1958, p. 106); and in including the pioneers of probation, "though these did not themselves add to the methodology of social work nor promote training for it" (p. 106, n. 1). Unless our journey into social work's past reveals something unique, socially creative, and integrated in that peak of 1903, it is clear that social work today faces a fourth historical option: to put the social into social work, rather than to keep looking backward to a tradition that gives little evidence of ever having existed.

Younghusband (1964) reports that some of the leading university teachers and social reformers of the early 1900s were on the committee of the C.O.S. School of Sociology, with economist Alfred Marshall serving as Chairman. Training was based on a combination of theory and practice, with major emphasis on direct experience under tutorial guidance. "Here, then, by the beginning of this century was all this hopeful activity in full flood."

> The vigorous and able members of the C.O.S. and its affiliated societies had discovered some of the main methods of casework, especially on the organizational side; the police court missioners, and the social welfare workers too, were experimenting with constructive personal relationships; the settlements under the leadership of their outstanding early wardens were active not only in their own neighbourhoods but also as centres of social research and were leaders in movements for social reform; and last but not least there was Octavia Hill with her understanding that housing, community development, casework and group work all belong together. There was training too. The settlements, Octavia Hill and the C.O.S. were from the 90s onwards the founders of social work education in this country. (p. 17)

According to Younghusband, the essential initial discoveries regarding the nature, processes, and methods of social work training had been made. "All seemed set for a steady advance into territory which had been soundly surveyed. Then for reasons which it is difficult to determine a blight set in, and, with one exception, social work in this country remained almost static, compared with the preceding half century, until after the second world war" (p. 18).

This period of early wisdom was indeed short-lived. Nine years after its inception, in 1912, the Charity Organisation's School of Sociology was joined with the London School of Economics to become the Department of Social Science and Administration. Lack of financial support was the main reason for the demise of the first school, which had some alliance with the social sciences.

It is not clear how quickly the "blight" set in. Younghusband, writing in 1953, spoke of the "darkness . . . of the past fifty years." Thus, it would appear that stagnation began immediately after the founding of the C.O.S. School.

By 1929, Younghusband reports, when the Commonwealth Fund of America began to sow the seeds of the child guidance movement in England—making possible both the first rays of light in the period of darkness and the training of England's most skilled social workers, the psychiatric—social work training clearly had fallen short of its early promise. It "had long since moved into the new university social science departments, where students were well educated in those basic subjects but with a relationship to the world of practice which became more tenuous as the years went by" (p. 18).

In the 50 years preceding World War Two, "there were immense advances made in social betterment; the foundations of the welfare state were slowly but steadily laid; and a great deal was discovered about how to eliminate poverty." Unfortunately, "social workers played almost no part in this and in social work itself there was nothing akin to the earlier advances and the earlier enthusiasm. Few people of the calibre of the early pioneers joined its ranks and no major discoveries were made about method or principles. The skill of the social worker was still mainly empirical, based upon intuition and common sense, and little was added to the existent body of knowledge. . . . Training too had reached a stage of stagnation compared with its early promise" (p. 18).

So it was that, almost as soon as it was attained, the peak of 1903 gave way to immediate stagnation. "Our School of Sociology died. We produced no Mary Richmond, no Gordon Hamilton, no Charlotte Towle, no standard books and practically no general literature on social work" (p. 19).

It is at this point that Younghusband looks enthusiastically to the integrated science-art contributions of United States social workers. She sees the postwar years as evidencing a profound change, especially "in the light (or against the darkness) of the past fifty years. Now the stagnation is ended and we are once more on the move, though slowly and painfully, realizing all the lost ground we have to regain" (p. 22).

Where Younghusband sees a groping back to a full tide of charted social activity, other views of social work's place in the ferment of ideas of the time show considerably more complexity.

As early as the 1880s, the ameliorist NAPSS, of which the C.O.S. was a member, had reached a crisis of understanding and action, "a different aspect of that broader intellectual crisis in which the statisticians and political economy as a whole were caught up by the inability of Victorian social science to make sense of the economic experiences of the 1870's" (Abrams, 1968, p. 49).

After 1885, the differences about the meaning of the social experience were too manifest to be ignored. "If there had ever been a single central tradition of social inquiry in Britain it was pulverized, as we have seen, in the critical years after 1873" (Abrams, 1968, p. 101).

In response to the recognition of the need for new solutions, previous avenues of commitment were in the process of reexamination and restructuring: politics, itself in the process of redefinition, was still open to the ameliorist; the government was sponsoring *ad hoc* social statistical investigation on an unprecedented scale; new political ideologies were being hammered out; and the skills of the economist and statistician were still in demand, even if their philosophy was in disrepute.

Added to this was the development of a new sociological consciousness. When Hobhouse offered sociology as a new synthesis in 1890, however, "it was open to question whether there could really be anything more than a desperate piecing together of intellectual interests whose real tendency was to fly off in a dozen different directions" (Abrams, 1968, p. 101).

The year in which the C.O.S. started its own School of Sociology, 1903, also saw the establishment of the Sociological Society in London, Europe's first national sociological association. At that time, however, it was not yet clear what sociology was, though it was loosely associated for many with Comte and Spencer's system building.

Even on the subject of the nature and goals of sociology, there was deep and pervasive disagreement among those inclined to abstract theory, those tending to piecemeal action, and those who sought to integrate the two positions. This same split was evident when the first courses in sociology were established in 1904 at the London School of Economics, leading to the establishment, in 1907, of a department of sociology, with Hobhouse and Westermarck as joint professors.

There was no golden age of integrated social science in 1903, and there could not have been a true age of borrowed wisdom for social work at that time. At most, social work's early wisdom was a glimmer of understanding that social work practice should somehow be related to the developing social sciences, whose own momentum was still divisive in 1914 (Abrams, 1968, p. 145).

Social work's School of Sociology was set up by Patrick Geddes, C. S. Loch, and others at the Charity Organisation headquarters, rather than as part of the attempt at sociological institutionalization at the London School of Economics. It is true that there was some interchange between the two centers. E. J. Urwick, for example, in 1909–10, gave lectures on Social Progress at the C.O.S. Center and, in 1912, when the C.O.S. School failed, became director of the separate Department of Social Science and Administration.

Urwick had been active both in the Sociological Society and the ameliorist NAPSS. In 1910, he was writing articles for the *Sociological Review* on such subjects as industrial statistics, the cost of living, school meals, town planning, trade boards for sweated industries, and starvation, as well as on the employment of married women, preventable disease, continuation schools for young workers, civic education for young women, imprisonment for debt, and the training of probation officers. Urwick was not interested in social structural theory. On the contrary, he is noted for "a sweeping and considered attack on the very idea of a general sociology: 'the claim of the general Sociologist is invalid at every point'" (Abrams, 1968, p. 111).

Patrick Geddes made important contributions to the development of sociology in Britain, especially in his advocacy of the survey as a potential tool. With age, however, he became increasingly eccentric, and he never "went much beyond indicating the most general outlines of the method of sociological surveys" (Abrams, 1968, p. 116). The influence of Loch remained pervasive, with his staunch defense of the C.O.S. against emerging views of poverty and its treatment.

Younghusband is justified in lamenting the break between theory and practice, but it is not clear why she sorrows that social work training "had long since moved into the new university social science departments . . . with a relationship to the world of practice which became more tenuous as the years went by." The new department of social administration was precisely an option in favor of the applied. Abrams comments that, understandable as it was, the separate institutionalization of sociology and social administration was a misfortune for both fields, threatening the already precarious integration of theory and practice.

Where Younghusband sees a happy coming together of social science and action in a floodtide of activity in the early 1900s, Abrams (1968) sees a split between the two which would require two world wars and five years of Labour government to mend before social structural analysis would become possible (p. 153).

Occasionally, social workers have complained that the problem of divorce between theory and action has been caused in part by the inability of social science in general, and sociology in particular, to make available concepts and frames of reference readily translatable into social action. The historical reality is more complex. Abrams notes that when a sociological tradition finally began to take shape in Britain, the entire social structure, including the university system, had been thoroughly shaken up. With the important exception of the work of T. H. Marshall, links to the sociology of the first generation were few; discontinuities, great; and many valuable resources for sociology, lost as a result (1968, p. 152).

Certainly, it is clear that, at the time of social work's professed "first wisdom," sociology was in disarray. What is not quite clear is why the social work profession did not see as natural allies those fragments of sociological inquiry that spun off from the commitment to scientific inquiry—efforts in the Geddes tradition of sociology, for example, less theoretically oriented than a future sociology, but more theoretically oriented than a social work divorced from main sociological currents. Booth, as another example, was neither involved in the Sociological Society nor concerned with grand theory, though he had come under the influence of Auguste Comte and positivism and "was fairly captivated" (Webb, 1926, p. 211). Yet his emphasis was in the sociological tradition.

Nor is it clear why the C.O.S. did not move in the direction of the churches, which it once had alienated, by incorporating some of the principles of Pope Leo XIII's "substantial contribution to the social thought of the late nineteenth century," his 1891 encyclical *Rerum Novarum*. The Pope saw the plight of the industrial worker as a social consequence of machine technology, a basic emphasis akin to that of Karl Marx, but with a radical difference in principle and perspective (Moody, 1961, p. 55).

Some 40 years ahead of the United States Supreme Court in denouncing the yellow-dog contract forbidding unionization, Leo's encyclical gave rise to a series of social encyclicals on the reconstruction of the social order according to Christian principles of justice. The culmination was the 1963 *Pacem in Terris* of Pope John XXIII, addressed to all men of good will and resulting in a series of international conferences.

In limiting themselves to a single option, said Webb, the C.O.S. forgot the experience of its forerunners, Chalmers and Edwin Chadwick, who eventually moved to support public provision of services strenuously. Chalmers became a champion of universal schooling, free if need be, and universal medical and surgical treatment. Chadwick, who had influenced the Poor Law Report of 1834, became an "infatuated . . . advocate" of positive municipal action within a decade of experience with the effects of the Poor Law (Webb, 1926, p. 198).

These developments were lost on Octavia Hill, C. S. Loch, and their immediate followers, who concentrated on schooling the poor "in industry, honesty, thrift and filial piety; whilst advocating . . . the moralization of the existing governing class, and its spontaneous conversion to a benevolent use of its necessarily dominant wealth and power" (Webb, 1926, p. 199).

If social work's accounts of its first wisdom are not quite convincing, neither are accounts of the ensuing dark age. The possibilities of choice for social work during this period were much richer than social work admits, just as the reality of sociology's attempts to institutionalize itself among Britain's social movements was much more difficult than social work appears to believe.

CURRICULUM: THE MINOTAUR LABYRINTH

The failure of American social work to be relevant to the needs of its clients because of an overriding interest in professionalization has its corollary in curricular requirements established by new associations pursuing the generic. The process bears a persistent similarity to the myth of the Minotaur.

Yet the schools for training social workers, as Klein observes, were from the very beginning the spiritual foundation on which the profession and early professional standards were built.

In 1919, four years after Dr. Flexner turned his attention to social work, 15 schools came together to form the American Association of Schools of Social Work. Membership was open to any educational institution which offered a full course of training extending at least one academic year and including substantial amounts of both class instruction and field work.

In 1919, the first school of social work was nearly 25 years old and had been offering a two-year sequence of training for some 10 years. "With few exceptions, the early schools, though created to meet a need for more thoroughgoing preparation than was possible on an apprenticeship basis, saw their purpose largely in terms of vocational training for specific agency tasks" (Kendall, 1953, p. 15).

Almost immediately after the formation of the AASSW, Kendall states, curriculum study became a major activity of the association, but it was not until 1930–31 that a curriculum committee was appointed to design some course of study that might be called "basic" for all schools engaged in social work training.

The Minimum 13

The first curriculum statement of the American Association of Schools of Social Work, issued in 1932, "went a step beyond vocational training. . . . The growing recognition of common knowledge and principles, particularly the concept of generic social case work, stimulated movement toward professional education" (Bartlett, 1959, p. 163).

The 1932 curriculum statement came to be known as the "minimum 13" because it defined 13 subjects as essential to a knowledge of social work. Three subjects were prescribed for the first year of instruction. Beyond that, there was some choice among the elements of "common knowledge and principles," as it was felt no school could require all students to take all 13 subjects in addition to field work in one academic year.

The new curriculum was designed to bring about a measure of standardization in social work training, to serve as an eligibility yardstick for membership in the association "in the light of the continuing struggle to arrive at 'some body of knowledge which may be called basic' " (Kendall, 1953, p. 16). The choices offered, however, were heavily weighted toward casework.

The 13 subjects were divided into three groups. Group A, required of everyone, included casework, medical information, and psychiatric information. Group B, from which two courses were required, included specialized casework, group work, and community organization. Group C and D were combined, with a choice of three out of eight offerings, including public welfare, child welfare, social legislation, social statistics, and social research. No effort was made to specify the content for the second year, on the assumption that the student would specialize in a functional field and take courses appropriate to that specialization.

Kendall (1953) comments: "We must recognize that it possessed within it the germ of basic preparation despite the compartmentalization of courses and the weighting in favor of social treatment. It was obviously intended that no student should finish the first year of social work training without some exposure to courses outside the 'core' area of case work, medical information, and psychiatric information" (p. 16).

The real core of "minimum 13," then, was the old C.O.S. casework, freshened by Freudian contact and medical exposure. From 1932 to 1944, this minimum curriculum stood as association policy, "although the association itself and many of its member schools had in the same period galloped far beyond it" (Kendall, 1953, p. 16).

The "Basic Eight"

Twelve years later, the "minimum 13" were replaced by the "basic eight," prescribed in 1944, after six years of preparation, "as the generic foundation for all professional practice" (Kendall, 1953, p. 16). The basic eight were: social casework, social group work, community organization, public welfare, social administration, social research, medical information, and psychiatric information. As far as possible, all courses were to be covered in the first year.

The committee, according to Kendall, was outlining areas of

knowledge rather than specific courses. "In practice, however, the statement tended to be taken too literally as a listing of courses, thus defeating the stated objectives of the committee" (pp. 16–17). As a result, says Kendall, although the "basic eight" proved valuable as an accreditation yardstick, the resulting uniformity carried dangers of its own. "The 'measure of similarity' which was so badly needed in fashioning the social work curriculum in the early years of professional education was to a large extent achieved through the 1944 curriculum policy statement. Unfortunately, the measure of similarity brought with it new dangers—the dangers of compartmentalized and fragmentary learning and of stereotypes and unimaginative curriculum design" (Kendall, 1953, p. 17).

Dissatisfaction with the "basic eight" brought a new "thoroughgoing" curriculum study and revision, adopted in 1952, closely following the monumental study by Hollis and Taylor (1951).

Hollis and Taylor postulated the need for a basic two-year course, but they saw little possibility of its achievement in less than a decade. They recommended making the first year of training genuinely and wholly basic in character.

More optimistic than Hollis and Taylor, the AASSW policy statement, whether wisely or unwisely, stressed the essential unity of the two-year curriculum: the first year should be devoted to the acquisition of beginning knowledge and skill; the second year would provide for extension of this knowledge and further development of skill. What might have been accomplished in 10 years was accomplished in one: the two-year program was to be considered essentially generic in nature.

Beginning and Its Extension

Criteria for social work's "beginning knowledge and skill" have embroiled social workers in agonizing discussion ever since. Despite disagreement, and without implementation of the Hollis-Taylor suggestion that criteria for entrance become a professional continuum, the 1952 curriculum policy statement came to be seen as a basic turning point in a generic two-year program.

The words *beginning* and *extension of beginning* were substituted for *generic* and *specific*, and it was urged that the entire program should form a unity. The AASSW policy statement dismissed the growing confusion over what was generic and what was specialized by making no reference to specializations.

All social work now had become generic.

The 1952 policy statement outlined the following broad areas of social work concern: (1) social services; (2) human growth and behavior; and (3) social work practice. The statement stressed community needs and change considerations.

In the same year, an AASSW Workshop added anthropology and

sociology to medicine, psychology, and psychiatry as relevant lending disciplines, although it offered no solution, as there is none today, to the problem of inserting these in a predominantly psychiatric body of information.

The 1962 Official Statement of Curriculum Policy for the Master's Degree Program in Graduate Professional Schools of Social Work in the United States and Canada, accredited by the Commission on Accreditation of the Council on Social Work Education, will be discussed later as a "milestone" recognition by the profession of its commitment to welfare and social amelioration aims. It is noteworthy that this 1962 statement of policy does not list generic elements, but broadly asks social workers to understand social structure, institutions, and the like.

The literature of social work today yields nothing remotely suggesting a valid statement of generic principles, although various approaches have been tried: calling beginning casework *generic* and advanced casework *specific*, calling the sequence of casework courses *generic*, and covering them in orderly progression over a two-year period.

Although needed research has not been conducted, specialized literature has been published. This, Bartlett (1959) feels, has advanced the understanding of the generic, but "too indirectly," with "no practice studies . . . focused on the common elements in social work" (p. 167).

New syntactical confusions have proliferated, with the profession taking an increasingly negative attitude toward previously valid specialization—valid on the assumption that each field of social work has unique features. Some persons have begun to see generic and specific as opposites "and to ask whether there was room for both in social work thinking" (p. 170). Bartlett laments that, with this overemphasis on the generic, which needed the concept of specialization to be valid, the entire concept of the generic was almost lost.

What should have been the merciful death of a tortuous discussion became instead a professional second breath. In 1952, the year of its organization as successor to the AASSW, the Council on Social Work Education took over the accreditation of specializations from separate organizations; in 1956, it decided to discontinue the accreditation of specializations. The Accreditation Commission asked major social work fields to analyze their practice to determine: (1) what specific content in terms of knowledge, skills, and attitudes is basic for all social workers; and (2) what specific content remains essential for professionally qualified workers in the field.

One year after the profession produced its 1958 "Working Definition of Social Work Practice," which Gordon (1965) calls "the most serious effort to provide a general perspective or frame of reference for the social work profession" (p. 20), generic courses already were offered in several British universities.

The American "Working Definition" notes that "significant and distinguishing elements of social work will be found in the values, the knowledge, the techniques, and the purposes of social work. . . . It does not say what these central values, knowledge, techniques, and other elements are, leaving these to be found or otherwise identified" (Gordon, 1965, p. 20).

By 1958, the pursuit of the generic had proceeded full circle back to Milford, 1923.

The Danger of Mystique

Wootton, for one, welcomed the development of the generic emphasis as representing a reaction against an extreme and narrow professionalism. The latter was one of the factors mitigating against the social work community in federal planning following the Depression.

She saw the generic emphasis as providing an opportunity for the social worker to acquire competence in more than one specialized field. The child welfare specialist and the probation officer, for example, could benefit from knowledge of the law—prophetic reasoning in view of the later Supreme Court *Kent* and *Gault* cases involving juveniles.

What Wootton feared—rightly—were implications of a "mastery" of a "mystique" of relationship behind the generic move. She feared that training courses would be designed not to impart a wider range of appropriate specialist knowledge, but to magnify out of all proportion those elements supposedly common to all casework.

> To those, however, who see "relationship" or the "helping process" as ancillary to the practical advice or help that the professional social worker (like the professional lawyer, architect, or accountant) can give, these common elements do not amount to much. Good manners, ability and willingness to listen, and efficient methods of record-keeping are the principal elements required. (Wootton, 1959, p. 291)

Wootton's fears were to be realized: "to the sponsors of generic courses for whom casework is one and indivisible, these [good manners and so on] are trivialities in comparison with the all pervading mystique of 'the relationship', descriptions of which adorn the social work manuals; and it is the mastery of this mystique, rather than the acquisition of any specialized practical knowledge, that is said to matter. As Donnison has said, summarizing the American attitude, 'To establish a "good relationship" with the client (and supervisor) marks a person as a good social worker. *Providing practical help and advice does not*' " (p. 291).

Social Work Valhalla

If Wootton is considered passé by the new breed of social work curriculum builders, her warning was still appropriate in 1965 when the *Journal of Education for Social Work* was launched. The dream of the generic still beckoned social workers, "the day when there are no separate method concentrations, but one Great Social Work Method" (Stein, 1965, p. 64).

Contradictions and confusions remain rampant. In the School of Social Service in which this author was involved, a "generic" course was launched, embracing two methods. I wish only that students had been spared one faculty member's belief that an example of community organization is sending a woman with breast cancer to a doctor. So pervasive is casework influence!

Smalley (1967) attests to a rapid development in the 1950s and 1960s of generic programs, "constituting core curricula to be required, for the most part of all students, with differentiation being confined almost entirely to method as taught in class and field rather than to field of practice" (p. 7).

At the time of Smalley's publication of *Theory for Social Work Practice*, in 1967, she reported some experimentation with teaching, if not a single method, two or more methods in a single practice class or sequence. She felt that the role of the Council on Social Work Education in the growth, improvement, and unification of social work education could not be overestimated.

Smalley devotes four chapters to a discussion of generic principles for social work, including five principles for social work practice generally, plus others for each of the three traditional methods, though she admits "the difficulty of finding a base for unity in identifying social work as a professional practice" (p. 1). For those interested in a 1967 understanding of generic principles, the pertinent four chapters of Smalley's work may be considered. The listing of five principles considered basic to all social work, derived from psychological, social, and process bases, serves to put the generic in its present perspective.

Principle I:
That diagnosis, or understanding of the phenomenon served, is most effective for all the social work processes which is related to the use of the service; which is developed in part, in the course of giving the service, with the engagement and participation of the clientele served; which is recognized as being subject to continuous modification as the phenomenon changes; and which is put out by the worker for the clientele to use, as appropriate, in the course of the service.

Principle II:
The effectiveness of any social work process, primary or secondary, is furthered by the worker's conscious, knowing use of time phases in the process (beginning, middles, and endings) in order that the particular potential in each time phase may be fully exploited for the other's use.

Principle III:
The use of agency function and function in professional role gives focus, content, and direction to social work processes, assures accountability to society and to agency, and provides the partialization, the concreteness, the "difference," the "given" which further productive engagement.

Principle IV:
A conscious, knowing use of structure as it evolves from and is related to function and process introduces "form," which furthers the effectiveness of all the social work processes, both primary and secondary.

Principle V:
All social work processes, to be effective as processes in social work, require the use of relationship to engage the other in making and acting on choices or decisions as the core of working toward the accomplishment of a purpose identified as own purpose, within the purpose of the service being offered. (Smalley, 1967, pp. 175–176)

No special insight or expertise is needed to observe that these principles say nothing about the content of the generic in social work's stock-in-trade. They simply conclude that social workers use relationship, ordinarily in an agency, in time, and with some consciousness that the world is made up of structures, in diagnosing the problems of clients, hopefully clients willing to be helped.

Pursuit of the "Will-o'-the-Wisp"

In two years, 1965–1967, the *Journal* contains only one negative comment by a contributor on the viability of the generic pursuit, and one review of a book questioning the generic reality in casework.

Eveline M. Burns, Ph.D., of the Columbia University School of Social Work, who admits to some 20 years of effort in dispelling the mystique, calls the profession's search for the generic a pursuit of a "will-o'-the-wisp." She has urged the profession to free itself from the ideological straitjacket of two major constraints: (1) the generic pursuit; and (2) the tendency to treat social policy as an afterthought because of a preoccupation with methods (1966, p. 18).

Despite her efforts, it is unlikely that social work will be able to make the transition from myth to reality easily: the pages of the *Journal* are replete with references to the generic, including a suggestion that generic content be made an elective in a doctoral program, which would make education a specific area of specialization.

The core course content identified earlier [as potential if not yet articulated] as essential preparation for social work education could be included as elective seminars without jeopardy to the core curriculum of the doctoral program. While experts from other professions may be called upon to assist us in this task, the development and teaching of this core curriculum in social work education must, of course, be carried out by social work educators. (Blackey, 1965, p. 9)

British Disagreement

The British, educator Noel Timms reports, are now at odds over the issues of generic social work education and practice. Timms observes: " 'Casework is never "generically" practiced,' " and, therefore, the caseworker is regarded not as " 'an expert in generalized problems of human relationships, but as a person trained to be "open" to these problems when they arise in the fulfillment of the functions of the agency.' " His *Social Casework*, according to reviewer Max Siporin, ends in a justification of the emphasis on agency function and the need to train students for "specialized," presumably beginning agency, practice (Siporin, 1965, p. 81).

Siporin objects to this viewpoint and to the second half of *Social Casework*, insofar as it is organized around the various fields of practice, because, "although much of the subject matter has generic implication, this is lost sight of when the material is presented out of its usual context" (p. 77). At the same time, he acknowledges many excellent points, including Timms's questioning of the status quo "in a modest, yet sometimes trenchant, way," and his observation that, because of the caseworker's fear of intellectualization, " 'the present state of social work literature reveals mainly an accumulation of unassorted ideas' " (pp. 77–78).

International Concern

Training for Social Work: Third International Survey (United Nations, 1958) reinforced generic concern: "a student of social work should have generic knowledge of the three methods of social work" and additional facility in the use of one method, used in a work setting. Acknowledging the importance of group work and community organization, the *Survey* regretted that these remained at a comparatively early stage so far as methodology, systematic practice, and case records for teaching were concerned (pp. 12–13, 42). The *Survey* recognized that, for the most part, students would be working in situations of mass poverty, which offered limited opportunity to use casework skills.

The *Survey* also discussed the difficult question of how much social workers needed to know about irrational behavior and unconscious motivation. It concluded that "such knowledge would become increasingly necessary as individualized services developed, for example probation and services for unmarried mothers."

An updating of the international viewpoint on the generic is provided by Dame Eileen Younghusband, President of the International Association of Schools of Social Work, who was welcomed to the pages of the *Journal* following a seminar on intercultural perspectives held at the University of Hawaii in 1966. Dame Younghusband (1966) concludes:

> Though the present three social work methods—casework, group work, and community work—are distinct, they are not necessarily separate. They have a common base; and any or all of them should be used flexibly in any given situation in whatever would be the most effective form of intervention. This raised the difficult question of whether students could be adequately trained in all three methods.... It is quite likely that casework is being over-emphasized in training at the expense of community work. This is partly because casework is very much better developed as a method by comparison with community work in which the clarification of practice skill and understanding of process is still weak. (p. 65)

The Reality Principle

The pursuit of the generic, will-o'-the-wisp or not, still prevails in modern social work. What becomes of the client in all of this?

Peter Berger has accused social work's doctrine of a singular obtuseness with regard to social reality. The literature gives no indication that the child Topsy has any intention of giving up the magic of the nonprofessional.

In its first year of publication, 1965, for example, the *Journal* contained only two articles that could be said to have anything to do with the reality principle of client needs. Both perceived reality so astigmatically that the title of one serves to suggest the thrust of both: "Through the Looking Glass: Adventure in Television" (Oswald, 1965).

The "Adventure" consisted in a two-year program at the School of Social Welfare at the University of California, Berkeley, "televising for use in teaching real social workers in their work with real clients" (p. 47). As in other social work literature, problems were overstressed and complexity increased well beyond the problems and complexities of everyday action: "Our experience in taping that session raised a pertinent question: should technical expert and subject expert try to achieve a symbiotic way of working? Or should the latter try to acquire the most relevant skills of the former? Specifically, since the social worker immediately knows on what aspect of a problem he wishes to focus, should he learn to be his own cameraman or his own camera director? Perhaps the question is not 'should he?' but 'can he?' " (p. 52).

The second article, "Enriching Social Work Education with Mental Retardation Content" (Dana, 1965), deals with the implications of the 1962 President's Panel on Mental Retardation for social work education. It is a classic example of the absurdity made possible by the magician who insists on doing public service by sleight of hand in lieu of professional reality appreciation.

> The Panel's belief that more people than the mentally retarded alone will benefit from a concerted national effort to prevent, treat, and ameliorate mental retardation ... presents social work educators with the far from simple task of determining how the practice insights emerging from an aggressive national movement to prevent and treat mental retardation can become an integral part of basic professional preparation *without*, on the one hand, diluting mental retardation content, and on the other, *violating the principles of generic education for general practice.* (p. 5, italics added)

Social work's fear of dilution of its generic content exists while "ways are still being sought to identify the common characteristics of all methods of intervention, whether directed toward changing the individual or the social conditions which constitute his world" (p. 8–9).

Nevertheless, "mental retardation content has been suggested for inclusion in the generic social work curriculum on the basis of its potential to inform or to inspire, to provoke question as well as to create certainty, to lend itself to new applications, and to underscore or illustrate old beliefs and accepted truths" (p. 10).

Finally, after listing five new insights by social workers regarding mental retardation, undistinguished except for their lack of sophistication and specificity, and outlining a tentative educational model for dealing with "chronicity," the article arrives at a conclusion startling in its fixation on social work's professional status rather than on the needs of the mentally retarded:

> Both in objectives and in content, help to the mentally retarded as it is now perceived reflects and supports the objectives of contemporary programs of graduate social work education and provides a rich resource for the selection of learning experiences through which these objectives are made operational. *Far from muddying the waters of generic education*, mental retardation content not only serves, but advances, the cause of learning to be a social worker *for which generic preparation stands.* (Dana, 1965, p. 10; italics added)

Social work's main contribution in response to the challenge of the President's Panel on Mental Retardation, apparently, is to offer mental retardates the opportunity to serve and advance the cause of learning to be a social worker in a generic program still looking for its core content.

ACADEMIC INCEST

Stimulated by the Depression and two world wars, American social work's mini-crusade for a return to the social had progressed by 1959 to the point where "material from the social sciences had been gaining greater recognition and acceptability" (Kadushin, 1959, p. 54).

Like its English counterpart, the American social work profession had not made any significant contribution to welfare gains in periods of national crisis, despite Younghusband's assessment that, when the Great Depression in the United States gave social workers the biggest opportunity in their history, "they rose to the challenge, they helped to form social policy and they learned how to apply the practice of social work to large scale public administration" (1964, p. 19).

In reality, observes Kadushin (1959), the cataclysmic events of the Depression and World War Two served merely to awaken social work to the need for the social. "The prolonged depression of the thirties had called insistent attention to the social environment. In itself, the depression did not seem to be sufficient to force a reorientation of social work. The depression was reinforced by the war. The social environment, once again, clamored to be recognized as a factor contributing to difficulties in social functioning. What the depression alone could not accomplish, the depression plus a war helped to achieve" (pp. 63–64).

Social workers in England played almost no part in the discovery of the effects of poverty and its structural alleviation. With individual exceptions, American social workers similarly did not include in their program the promotion of social insurance as a new and more efficacious way of dealing with poverty. As a group they were not active in seeking enactment of America's first Social Security Act, nor any subsequent social legislation. If American social workers " 'brought the intensity of need to the attention of the nation and its lawmakers and . . . influenced the content of the developing program' " of the Federal Emergency Relief Administration, as noted by Eveline Burns, a severe critic of social work's failure to initiate social policy (Beck, 1959, p. 199), their rising to the challenge, with few exceptions, did not include promoting social insurance (p. 200).

Again, if social work showed " 'great ability and flexibility in mobilizing its resources to help defeat axis powers,' " as Nathan E. Cohen maintains, "social work's contribution remained limited as it pertained to questions of broad policy in the development of social services to meet the needs of a nation at war" (Beck, 1959, p. 200).

By the end of the 1950s, even with a slight movement toward the social, the ratio of borrowed to indigenous social work knowledge still was heavily weighted in favor of the psychoanalytic in the third basic area of the social work curriculum, as defined by the Council on Social Work Education: "Human Growth and Behavior." In this area, where the social work student was now to be presented with a social viewpoint, "we owe the greatest indebtedness by far . . . to psychoanalytic psychology or its derivative. From it we derive our principal knowledge and understanding of normal and abnormal personality development, the dynamics of normal and abnormal behavior, the anatomy of personality, and the mechanisms of adjustment" (Kadushin, 1959, p. 54).

The historical tendency to tribal isolation and the more modern tradition of academic incest are not easily overcome, even with new curriculum requirements espousing learning of the social. "Human Growth and Behavior" does not automatically become social structural learning by virtue of its title, especially if taught as an extension of psychiatry, or by a psychiatrist-social work team.

As late as 1964, Florence Hollis was writing:

> These sociological data amplify the rich understanding of the internal dynamics of the personality developed by the Freudian school of thought; they do not replace it. . . . Casework will drastically impoverish itself if it follows the lead of Horney and Sullivan in trying to explain human behavior primarily in interpersonal terms, omitting those key intrapsychic phenomena that from the start influence the child's perception of and reaction to his interpersonal experiences. But it can use the insights of sociologists as additions to the knowledge of the inner life of the child uncovered by Freud. (p. 11)

It has been said, Hollis adds, that casework is directed toward the social side of adjustment and psychiatry to inner psychological adjustment, "but this is a false distinction. Although certain branches of psychiatry explore regions of intrapsychic functioning which casework does not investigate, casework characteristically must deal with mental processes, and psychiatry with interpersonal material" (p. 11).

Putting the Social Back

Whenever social work returns to the task of putting the social back into social work, one is reminded of the indefatigable pioneer of social casework, Mary Richmond, who, tradition has it, was responsible for an early insistence that the social be put back into casework.

It was Mary Richmond who reportedly lamented that she spent half her life insisting that social casework was legitimate in social work, and the other half insisting that it was not all of social work. It is to this author of *Social Diagnosis* (1917) that the profession turns when it runs out of ancestors who, according to myth, have espoused the social, or social thinkers who are only mythically ancestors of social work. It is Mary Richmond's name that is summoned out of history as part of the great American hope not achieved in the early years of British social work. "Our School of Sociology died," writes Younghusband. "We produced no Mary Richmond . . ." (1964, p. 19).

Mary Richmond was not as social as slogans attributed to her may sound, certainly not social enough to be counted among social structural reformers. Nor are American social workers as scientifically grounded in the social as Younghusband sees them:

> Fundamentally the great advances made by the Americans came from the work of Mary Richmond and from the application of dynamic psychology as the scientific foundation underlying the techniques of social work; while we continued to rely on the study of academic psychology in the class room and unadulterated intuition and common sense in the field. The difference is that the Americans took hold of what the scientific study of living human beings had to tell them. . . . They used all this knowledge in their practice of social work and added to it and they reduced the whole to consistency and coherence so that they could teach it to others. In short, they have used organizational method and applied scientific knowledge as the basis for developing the professional practice of social work. (p. 19)

Selectively Social

Mary Richmond's notion of the social was personally selective, and, as late as the 1960s, in social work's latest return to the social, even Mary Richmond's limited vision of the social often has been denied. Examples of the ambiguity and ambivalence in the modern return to the social are not difficult to find.

In the fourth edition of *The Field of Social Work* (1963), the authors admit:

> Practically all the foregoing discussion was based upon the one to one relationship that exists between the client and the psychiatrist or the client and the psychiatric social worker. Increasingly, however, it is becoming clear that help can also be offered through a relationship involving the psychiatrist or psychiatric social worker and a group of clients or patients. This is not to be confused with the usual range of activities carried on with groups by workers in group work agencies. Rather it is a recognition that the lives of most of us are lived in

groups, and that what is termed socialization of the individual takes place essentially through group activity. (Fink, Wilson, and Conover, p. 264)

If social work now recognizes that most of us are socialized in groups, the profession, according to this statement, still has not recognized that most of us do not internalize our value systems from psychiatrically therapeutic or social work-oriented groups, and, consequently, that not every problem or deviance needs a psychiatric solution.

The two final chapters of *The Field of Social Work* are devoted to "Social Group Work" and "Community Organization for Social Welfare."

In a more recent attempt to develop a social work theory, *Theory for Social Work Practice* (1967), Smalley prefaces her work with the reminder that "the segment of the profession concerned with communities, either through community organization or community development, is just now struggling to identify a method that rests on a theory for practice" (p. ix). "No attempt will be made to give 'equal time' to the group and to the community, as phenomena served by group or community workers, in comparison with what has been developed for the individual" (p. 89), for two reasons: the lesser development of the group and community client systems and the author's own lesser familiarity with the terrain.

In 1968, one year short of the centennial of its founding, social work's approach to the social through its group and community organization techniques was characterized by Klein as: (1) actually not existing, in the case of group work; and (2) handled principally in the voluntary field, and so treated in the curriculum, in the case of community organization (p. 175).

However insistent social work's present claims for a return to the social, certain countertrends, including the sheer weight of previous historical choice, do not justify the profession's rather haughty response to critics that social work's failure to incorporate the social should be relegated to ancient history. Social work's handling of its problem with the social is yet another example of a coping mystique.

Hollis and Taylor, in their 1951 report, *Social Work Education in the United States*, emphasized faculty preoccupation with social work education shaped to the needs of private social welfare agencies. To whatever degree the criticism was merited then, it is a mark of our progress that it sounds like ancient history today. There is strong impetus within social work education today to give the public field its proper place and to see the function of social work in increasingly broader terms. (Stein, 1965, p. 57)

Optimistic as this may seem, the fact remains that professional social workers comprised less than one-fifth of personnel in social welfare in 1960 (Klein, 1968, p. 209). Some four-fifths of social welfare problems are left to the judgment of the untrained or those who have had only minimum contact with social work's identity crisis, growing pains, and search for the social.

In 1966, Mark P. Hale, describing current manpower shortages, indicated a need for 10,000 to 12,000 social workers to fill continuously vacated budgeted positions, an additional 12,000 to 15,000 to meet expanded service demands, and 5,000 to 8,500 for retirement replacements. Hale projected a need by 1970 for 21,000 social workers in public aid, 12,000 in child welfare, and 11,500 in juvenile delinquency services (pp. 33–34). In view of social work's very real shortages of manpower, the researcher into social work's past can sympathize only in part with social work's continuing difficulties with the social.

Wootton's 1959 assessment still seems eminently applicable, when she comments on "the current American demand for 'putting the "social" back into social work'—a slogan which might mean much or little, though I must confess that, until writers on social work substitute more concrete language for their habitually misty vocabularies, I am myself left in some doubt as to what it does mean" (p. 287).

The countermovement toward the social, Wootton writes, seems to imply, first, a relaxation of hitherto popular attempts to imitate psychoanalysis "and, second, realization of such facts as that families live in streets amongst neighbours, not in a vacuum, that much of most lives is spent in factories or other workplaces, and that people are affected by what happens outside their homes as well as by their domestic relationships."

> Some of this criticism may presage a radical change of attitude. It is refreshing, for instance, to find Miles frankly lamenting the fact that "so many groups in our society feel compelled to elevate their status by using a meaningless mumbo jumbo to frighten the uninitiated." As yet, however, the facade, at once defensive and pretentious, by which social work seeks to justify its professional existence, has not been seriously shaken. (p. 287)

The Fourth Historical Option

If, as Wootton (1959) concludes, social work's criticism of its own contemporary trends does not yet amount "to much more than tentative murmurs" (p. 284), countervailing trends are very much in evidence. Whether or not social work has come of age, as the *Journal* proclaimed in 1965, the profession cannot be a part of the 20th-century helping disciplines without recognition of the social and due incorporation of social insights. If it is not too late already, now is the time for social work's fourth major historical option: the unequivocal embrace of social theory.

If, right from its inception, "the Society [C.O.S.] had one eye cocked to its casework, the other to the wider questions affecting the conditions of the poorer classes in London" (Woodroofe, 1962, p. 60), then now is the time to avow formally that the Society's one eye cocked to wider social conditions always has been severely astigmatic and that modern accounts about a return to the social reflect a need for optical correction.

How social work responds to the present historical choice will determine whether the school of social work in 1990 will indeed have become "a hospitable center and intellectual home for all of the great array of occupations, professional, subprofessional, and technical, that make up the field of social welfare broadly conceived" (Gardner, 1966, p. 7).

In addition, social work's current decision will determine whether the new school of social work will see a transformation of the work of volunteers—that new modern army ready to do battle with problems social—whose work in social service is older than the profession of social work itself.

In the process of its development as a hospitable center and intellectual home for social sciences and services, says Gardner, the school of the future will include the following characteristics: (1) a commitment to conducting its own appraisal of social needs and problems, as well as of methods by which social services are delivered and institutional arrangements through which people's needs are met; (2) intimate and continuing ties with agencies that provide social services, even if the latter bear little relationship to present-day agencies; (3) provision for innovation and exchange, more highly developed than at present, with behavioral and social science fields in the university; and (4) a rejoining of forces by schools of social work and social agencies to provide far better arrangements than exist today for the continuous renewal of the field.

How well is social work responding to the challenge of academic openness?

Although social work recognizes, at least verbally, that casework, with its psychoanalytic orientation, is not getting client results, no part of the field has produced a comparable amount of literature, and discarding one's past and present is not easy.

Even with the help of attacks on the validity of Freudian psychoanalysis from other quarters, measuring casework's usefulness to the client over time would require painful professional honesty and would keep curriculum pronouncements in a state of abeyance for an uneasy period. "Even if such analysis were technically feasible," observes Klein (1968), "the required manpower and lack of intellectual commitment by the casework world would cancel it" (p. 171).

Consequently, there are discouraging signs that the effort will not materialize beyond the point of insisting that the process has

begun—or is already finished. Kadushin (1965) says: "It is significant that those who advocate primary prevention as an appropriate
role for social work define it as building an intra-psychic immunity
to social stress in individuals by intervention at developmental
crisis points in order to prevent interpersonal problems from arising" (p. 46).

With the roots of social work's alliance with psychiatry a half-
century in the ground, pretensions of social workers to being junior
psychiatrists will be relinquished only with anguish. It is logical to
suspect that reactions to suggestions that this method be examined
for effectiveness would meet with the same dismay exhibited by
psychiatrists faced with evidence of Freudian deficiencies — as
Eysenck (1966) suggests, with the horror one would encounter if
proposing that the efficacy of prayer be analyzed by statistical
methods (p. 5).

By way of example, Kadushin (1965) softens the blow for social
work in one of his conclusions:

> One does not have to wholly accept Eysenck's negative conclusions as
> stated in his recent comprehensive review of research on the effects of
> psychotherapy, nor Leavitt's equally negative, but better balanced,
> comprehensive review of the research on the results of psychotherapy
> with children. Yet the reviews inevitably leave one chastened with re-
> gard to how many people are helped, and to what degree, by intensive
> casework. (p. 41)

The reader is offered no clue as to why Leavitt's book should be
considered better balanced than Eysenck's, and it may well be that
feeling chastened will be found to be equivalent to being on firmer
empirical treatment ground.

What is generally apparent in the literature is social work's pervasive fear of the social sciences.

> Coyle points to the danger of "confusion of identifications which seem
> to be a common result of inter-professional borrowing"—a confusion
> which is intensified when we borrow teachers as well as knowledge
> from the "lending" discipline. There are even now occasional warnings
> that we will have only a minor achievement if we move from being
> little psychiatrists to being little social scientists. (Kadushin, 1959, pp.
> 68–69; Coyle, 1958, p. 12)

Behind that fear is an evident unfamiliarity with the material of
the social sciences, which will not be dissipated by insisting that
social workers pick and choose from the lending discipline. As late
as 1964, in a paper on "The Place and Use of Knowledge in Social
Work Practice," Bartlett makes the incredible claim that social work
already operates on knowledge peculiar to social work (p. 45).

Apparently, there is some professional satisfaction to be derived
from asserting the short distance to be traveled. "Social workers do
not have to move far when they move from an orientation focused
on psychoanalytic psychology to one which borrows more liberally

from contemporary social sciences" (Kadushin, 1959, p. 61). "The personality, clinical, and therapeutic orientation is still dominant. Social science material is being used primarily to enhance a more comprehensive understanding of personality development and behavior rather than to reemphasize social action (p. 64).

Kadushin's discussion of social science and social work is a good example of social work ambivalence and misunderstanding of the nature of both areas—the art of social work and the science of the lending discipline. "My own guess is that we are apt to be disappointed in the knowledge borrowed from social science because it deals with questions relative to the social sciences rather than questions formulated by social work" (p. 73).

Again, in showing the natural harmony of psychiatry and the social sciences, Kadushin explains: "Two leading American sociologists stated that 'in the deepest sense our debt is to the work of the great founders of modern social science, among whom we may single out Durkheim, Freud and Max Weber'" (pp. 60–61). The distance between Durkheim and Freud, however, is longer than Kadushin would prefer to believe.

Meanwhile, the decidedly contradictory account of how social social work has ever been keeps recurring as a falsely reassuring theme.

Herbert Bisno, in "How Social Will Social Work Be?" (1956), sees social work's quest for professional status as tending to turn it away from earlier social action programs. If these trends continue, he feels, it is likely social work will continue to de-emphasize controversial social action and will come to accept a role of technician-implementer (pp. 12–18).

Nathan E. Cohen (1958) sees the decline of social reform in social work as occurring between World War One and the Depression, as a reflection of the general cultural movement away from an emphasis on social reform toward a search for normalcy after the war (p. 138).

Beck (1959), while not denying the existence of these trends, views their consequences more optimistically. He cites a time toward the end of the 19th century as the beginning of social work's consciousness of itself, if not as a profession, then as a social force. Out of this interest in social reform, which characterized social work until the First World War, came notable advances in court reform, improved housing, recreational facilities, and health measures.

During this time of social consciousness, schools of social work also were concerned with providing students with a base for understanding social and economic problems. In fact, Beck adds, early in social work's history, one of the first schools weathered a difference of opinion as to the degree to which the school would prepare students for day-to-day work with clients as against understanding of broad social forces. "The conflict was resolved in terms of the needs of the agencies, but this merely meant a more balanced curriculum relating the study of social problems to the helping task; it did not mean an abandonment of social policy tasks" (p. 194).

One of the advantages of such magic talk is that it offers no constraint toward consistency or precision. Thus, Beck is able to conclude:

> The trends described by Mr. Bisno and others are not such as will vitiate social work's role as a determinant of social policy; but rather they are such as will strengthen and refine that role. These trends have the potential, at least, of allowing social work, not to make so rigorous a contribution as was made by the early pioneers but certainly to make a unique one. . . . Social work's future need not be . . . a sharp break with its social action-oriented past but rather a logical continuation from the past gaining vitality—and not repeating old errors. (p. 193)

Perpetual Childhood

The cost of introducing scientific concepts into the social work curriculum is high. New ideas are monitored by a supposedly benevolent social work special knowledge; the intruder is consigned to the status of academic enemy, caseworked by the wisdom of the child of social work itself, Topsy—because, as Topsy knows, the possibility of precipitous error in the field of the social is always with us.

> One of the intellectual hazards of our time might be called "seduction by computer." . . . The researcher who feeds the machine has learned a difficult language, one that brings him into easy communication with certain academic fields and carries the probable rewards of promotion and tenure. But the language may carry an attendant shift in values that leads to alienation from social work practice. (Schubert, 1965, p. 41)

In "Social Science and Social Work: A Theory of Their Relationship" (1955), Ernest Greenwood offers two reasons why collaborative research between social scientists and social workers should be conducted in social work's own setting:

> First, to perform research on the social work process, social scientists must have access to the operations of the social work practitioner. Second, research programs so located can be better controlled by social workers. Such control is very important, to avoid having social scientists formulate research questions in a manner that might impair their relevance for social work practice. (p. 31)

By 1958, some form of social science had been incorporated into the curricula of 52 accredited schools of social work, comprising "a considerable body of knowledge drawn from sociology and anthropology" (Coyle, 1958, p. 25). According to Eaton (1956), until "recently training in general personality theory was largely restricted to psychoanalysis. Since World War II, however, other behavior science approaches are being added" (p. 15).

By 1959, a number of workshops at annual meetings of the Council on Social Work Education had been devoted to the cultural component in the social work curriculum.

> Some agencies are beginning to use social scientists as consultants, and schools of social work frequently include on their faculties social workers who have advanced training in the social sciences. The doctoral programs of social work frequently offer a heavy concentration of social science courses. (Kadushin, 1959, p. 60)

Official Recognition of Social

The profession implicitly recognized social work's dual concerns—the effect of society on the individual and the clinical concern with individual personality—in *Goals of Public Policy*, formally adopted at the Association's first Delegate Assembly and revised in 1958 and 1962 (National Association of Social Workers, 1963).

Both Louis Lowy (1960) and Eveline Burns (1961) have suggested that the profession's goals must be translated into effective curriculum programming. Lowy says that NASW goals of public social policy will remain mere lofty aspirations unless given "instrumentalities for achievement," and asks for a return to the concept of "social statesmanship." He also advocates socializing students in social action by providing that foundation upon which knowledge of society can be built (pp. 99–100). Burns proposes a specific curriculum to provide this specialized knowledge and skill (pp. 23–24).

In 1962, the Council on Social Work Education issued an *Official Statement of Curriculum Policy for the Master's Degree*, recognizing the need to alert students to the broad goals of public policy and to encourage the study of social structure.

Examination of the 1962 proposal, however, indicates that the directive is, at best, only general in nature, with no clear-cut curriculum proposals. The curriculum is envisioned as a unified whole, with three major components: Social Welfare Policy and Services, Human Behavior and the Social Environment, and Methods of Social Work Policy, each subdivided into its various contributions to goals of student learning. The categories are vague and overlapping, and tend to confuse values and social content.

The official statement also encounters difficulty in assigning discrete meanings to such words as "understand," "recognize," and "identify." This difficulty follows from the notion that, for each item introduced into the curriculum, the precise value to be conveyed to the student must be tagged appropriately. With a certain similarity of social work values implied in the introduction of different types of social work material, curriculum planners soon run out of discrete value categories. Under Human Behavior and the Social Environment, for example, one set of objectives has been assigned to help students "understand and develop"; the second category, to help students "recognize, understand, and appraise." There is no question that a computer would have difficulty.

Human Behavior and the Social Environment

The section on Human Behavior and the Social Environment is a good example of social work's official struggle today with the problem of the social, although the entire *Official Statement* should be read to appreciate fully the paucity of clear directional content.

This area of content is designed to help the student:

Understand the essential wholeness of the human being, and recognize the interaction of physical, intellectual, emotional, spiritual, and social influences and attributes.

Understand the influence of social structures (e.g. families, groups, organizations, communities, and societies) and social processes on the behavior of individuals and on groups and communities.

Develop a basis for objective assessment of those whom the social worker serves through knowledge and understanding of:

the individual's capacity for effective social functioning;

the dynamics of groups of varied composition and in varied settings, and the significance of the group for its members;

the forces in the community that bear on human welfare and on relationships between ethnic, religious, and other groups in the community. (Council on Social Work Education, 1962, p. 4)

The second category in this major component of student knowledge "should enable the student to recognize, understand, and appraise":

The processes of growth and personality development of the individual within the social contexts of the family, group relationships, occupational settings, and community structures.

Human behavior in the light of personal and cultural norms and values and varying conceptions of effective social functioning and well-being.

Behavior of the individual under stress, with attention to maturation, growth, development, and environmental influences and of his use of adaptations and defenses.

Sources and manifestations of deviant behavior and social pathology.

Disease and disability as they affect social functioning.

The varied and changing nature of the key roles which individuals carry, and the positive or negative influences of these roles on the behavior of the individual in his interpersonal, group, and organizational relationships.

The nature and changing character of social and cultural structures, with attention to the interaction between the individual and his social environment, and the reciprocal effects of the interaction. (pp. 4–5)

There is no doubt that all social bases have been touched in this official statement of purpose. The question is how they tie in with psychiatric underpinnings. From the author's experience in a school of social service undergoing curricular reorganization, it is quite possible to be pro-social in name and an old-time social caseworker in practice. In this instance, after one year of study and committee work, "putting back the social" had been translated into some discussion of role and family and an enthusiastic, if wildly inappropriate, dedication of effort to the support and preservation of the "nuclear" family.

Social purpose can become mere window dressing for previous assumptions. Barbara Varlay's (1963) interpretation of the new social directive is a case in point. Describing the value of "psychodynamic-mindedness," in an experimental study of the assimilation of social work values by beginning and graduating social work students, she concludes that all responses to stress and related problems can be explained in terms of "personality differences, of deviations from the normal patterns of growth and development." Therefore, "treatment of clients . . . is assumed to be of major importance in social work, while social action and institutional change are basically of secondary importance" (pp. 102–104).

By 1967, the notion of incompatibility between social work and social science was being voiced again. Discussion Paper No. 2, presented by Britain's Council for Training in Social Work, states in its Foreword to "Human Growth and Behaviour—As a Subject of Study for Social Workers":

The course of study which in social work training is usually called Human Growth and Behaviour is one about which there is much controversy but with insufficient discussion of the very real issues. Some critics are skeptical about the mixture of knowledge, theory and speculation which is contained in the literature and teaching on what they regard as "not a subject at all." Others view with alarm the inclusion of teaching from experimental psychology and from sociology which they sometimes regard as unrelated to understanding "real people." (Council for Training in Social Work, p. 1)

And Mary Richmond

If experimental psychology and sociology are suspected of being somehow unrelated to understanding "real people," how relevant to real people was the maverick to the professional social work scene, Mary Richmond? Indeed, how social was this largely self-taught advocate of a return to the social, who began her work under the auspices of a C.O.S. framework and its attendant assumptions?

On several occasions, Mary Richmond insisted that "social reform and social casework must of necessity progress together. We have seen, for example, the diagnostic side of casework received a great impetus when the plans of the reformers began to be realized" (1917, p. 365).

There is no doubt that Mary Richmond did engage in community reform. She had reservations, however, about giving public funds for mothers' pensions, for fear that husbands would be encouraged to desert. "Thus Mary Richmond broke with many of her colleagues on the issue of movement forward toward public responsibility, and took a stand with which we are not in sympathy" (Towle, 1961, p. 388).

Though Mary Richmond, more than any other single caseworker, changed the purpose of a social study from a means of protecting donors against impostors to a scientific study of the situation, "she was still influenced by John Glenn's idea of the ideal agent as a detective" (Pumphrey, 1961, p. 385). As a result, she did not see the contradiction of an investigation that proceeded without full client awareness of the steps being taken.

"In keeping with the original institutional purpose of C.O.S. of preventing duplication and promoting coordination of the work of all agencies, she initiated community conferences, urged more general use of the C.O.S. Registration Bureau (later the Social Service Exchange), and campaigned for better investigation of applicants for relief and service" (p. 380).

Convinced of the need to generalize findings, and hopeful that success could be duplicated consistently with the accumulation of more fact on client cases, "she saw investigation as the first part of the process and dealt with it as a scientifically minded perfectionist, determined to overlook no detail" (p. 384). At one point, she became so compulsive about insisting that every obtainable fact about the client's past and present be compiled that some of her visitors described feeling almost like policemen.

The Dilemma Remains

From Loch to Richmond to the present, social work's dilemma with the social continues, with neither society nor the social work curriculum substantially changed by the struggle. There is at the moment, nevertheless, a feeling of avant garde experimentation among social workers. Kadushin (1965), for example, points to "Thomas' brave attempt at programmed teaching of role theory at the University of Michigan School of Social Work" (p. 40). The bravery is considerably overstated, except if attributed to the client.

Beck (1959), as a final example, laments that, up to 25 or 30 years ago, sociology's efforts to explain social change lacked a scientific base, and then makes the uncanny choice of Toynbee's discussion of the downfall of the elite to illustrate sociological theory's potential for social work's social change movement.

> Seen in the light of Toynbee's formulation, social work's unique role in social change might be not simply to advance measures of social reform which embody those values—for there are many who will do this—but through the application of social work methods to check forces of barbarism in individual, group, and community. (p. 204)

PRIESTS AND PROPHETS

The preference of social work for the role of functionary over that of visionary has severely limited its professional leadership in large-scale reform. Nevertheless, the priest-versus-prophet theme has occupied the literature for over 30 years.

In point of fact, as Henry Meyer (1959) has noted, the profession may not be permitted to abandon either approach. "Expertness in the one may well require expertness in the other, for the profession as a whole, if not for each professional social worker as an individual" (p. 333).

How does social work see its role of prophet, or the abandonment of its minimal institutional prophetic role, which is a more accurate statement of the question in view of the profession's history? As late as 1964, for example, among students at the University of Wisconsin who participated in an education and voter registration drive in Mississippi, only one had contact with social work. She left the school of social work after one semester, "dissatisfied with the lack of implementation by our faculty of our verbal expression of concern with social problems" (Kadushin, 1965, p. 45, n. 43).

Kadushin (1965) states: "Both 'function' and 'cause' are appropriate for the profession. There is no real conflict between the 'priest' and the 'prophet.' But the profession has found it easier to educate 'priests' to perform 'functions' rather than 'prophets' to implement 'cause.' This is because we have been able to develop the change agent principles and skills which would enable the practitioners to perform 'function.' We have not as yet developed the 'procedures' that would enable 'prophets' to implement 'cause'" (p. 43).

The Quest for Values

At an international conference held in 1966, social workers representing various cultures still were fidgeting about their place in social functioning and their unique values, "a constantly recurring theme all through the discussions."

"Quite early in the seminar it was agreed that social work is committed to social change. This was defined as 'change for the better' but although participants kept on coming back to it, they never came to grips with what was meant by better" (Younghusband, 1966, p. 61).

This intercultural gathering made various attempts to list values,

> in the sense of human needs, like a rising standard of living or desires like liberty or equality, but with recognition of problems that arise from the clash between values and the dilemma of "what trumps what." This dilemma included the clash between professional and culturally held values. Such a clash occurs, for example, in circumstances where it is assumed that one should get jobs for one's relatives or where one's professional values conflict with the tenets of one's religion. (p. 61)

The discussion, as is evident, was at the most elementary level of professional awareness. Participants repeated the ubiquitous call for incorporation of knowledge from the social and behavioral sciences, and the equally ubiquitous fear that such incorporation would threaten social work values. Thus, "the growth and application of scientific knowledge, particularly in the social and behavioral sciences," intensified "the need for professional value commitments in order to protect the individual, group, or community from manipulation and exploitation" (p. 61).

If social work has a responsibility to protect society's values, the attempt to define these values is hardly encouraging: "Because nothing was taken for granted, it looked at times as though nothing would be left but a few vague generalizations. The group went through the normal process of analyzing, discussing, and going around in circles" (p. 59).

> It was agreed that the ultimate aim of social work is the well being of the individual human being, that nothing should be done to diminish his humanity and everything possible done in the given circumstances to enhance it. As one member put it: "It isn't possible to analyze this value further; it is a value at the end of the line, and one can only assent with a grunt." (p. 60)

Even this broad generalization, however, immediately led to another problem:

> Should the social worker give expression to his values or only encourage the client to express his, in the hope that sooner or later he will arrive at those of the social worker? This specter of skillful manipulation, of forcing men to be free, of "Daddy knows best" kept floating across all the discussion. (p. 61)

Other definitions of social work's place in the social helping scene, though more complex, have proved no more enlightening:

> As a technology we are concerned with achieving "controlled changes in natural relationships via relatively standardized procedures that are

scientifically based." As a species of the genus technology, practice is concerned with changes in human beings. As the subspecies social work, in the species practice, in the genus technology, we are concerned with changes in the social relationships of human beings. (Kadushin, 1959, p. 69; Greenwood, 1955, p. 24)

In summary, whatever the status of prophetic social work values, and even though no value system has been discovered, optimism remains undimmed. At the same time, fear of the social sciences as a threat to values may inhibit borrowing from them in the future. We are left with the image of Toynbee's barbarians at the door, held at bay by a professionally confused elite.

So much for prophets.

The Quest for Function

"Function . . . gave the group as much trouble as values" in 1966. It was clear that the social work function differs in different parts of the world. Nonetheless, it was felt that the similarities were sufficient for the same profession to be recognizable everywhere. Neither differences nor similarities were objectified, however, and the group concluded that "social work is a fluid and emerging profession, and like many other professions, it is not stable either at its center or at its circumference" (Younghusband, 1966, p. 61).

However difficult it may be to conceive of a professional social system stable neither at its center nor its circumference, the conference concluded that: "Social work has a cluster of activities and values that are not exclusive in content but in configuration; while its aims and methods are not identical with those of any other profession" (p. 62).

Historically, the social work educators affirmed, social work began as a social movement, "but is now developing more clear professional functions and methods. Because of its heavy commitment to certain social values and to social betterment, it is desirable that it should continue to have a social reform element in it" (p. 62).

The social work function "was variously defined" as:

an endeavor to do something rational in the field of social living; to enable people to be able to function more adequately on their own behalf in relation to social problems; to promote socially constructive and personally gratifying transactions between individuals, groups, and communities, including an improvement in their circumstances; and to generate in individuals a capacity to meet multiple role demands. (p. 62)

Social workers in 1966 also agreed to come into action where breakdown of role performance occurs: "in crisis situations . . . and in conditions of violent social change, such as disaster, urbanization, mass migration, or drastic innovation (for example, the social consequences of building a dam)" (p. 62). In all cases, however, the commitment to therapeutic amelioration was implied, despite former failures. The social commitments of social work "all imply direct service of an individual or social therapy type; indeed, the therapy function of social work is the most highly developed so far" (p. 62).

So much for priests and functionaries.

Whatever fascination inheres in the over-30-year-old discussion about respective roles of prophet and priest, two conclusions persist: (1) Social work has not been prophetic as a profession, however impressive the performances of such individual social workers as a Jane Addams. (2) Starting as a method branch of secular humanism, social work as of 1966 gave no evidence of moving toward a broader political and religious value orientation, as demonstrated in the civil rights movement of the 1960s, or as envisioned earlier in Mary Elizabeth Walsh's *Saints and Social Work* (1937).

Early Wisdom

There is evidence, however, to substantiate social work's claim to periods of "early wisdom"—times when social insights were grasped more fully. These formally acknowledged periods, as we have seen, were of relatively short duration and not always as "social" in the structural sense as social workers seem to believe.

What social work generally does not admit to having lost are certain periods of its history when functioning was closer to the reality demands of the respective situation.

Whether or not one agrees with the perspective of the progenitors of social work, the characters involved in the Charity Organisation Society are believable in retrospect, and they were clear about their function and value system: separating the deserving poor from the undeserving poor to prevent monetary and social waste. Similarly, social work's ancient clients also were distinguishable, if only by their abject misery. Social work's first clients were believable in much the same way that Frederic M. Thrasher's gang boy of 1927 often seems more believable than later sociological constructions (Bordua, 1961).

First School of Social Work

In contrast to 20th-century professional vagueness and indecision on the questions of who and what are the social worker and the client, the program of "the first real school of social work in the world," started in Amsterdam in 1899 as the Institute for Social Work Training, made it quite clear what the social worker was to be doing and, by implication, who the client was.

Modern social workers admit that the program, even by today's standards of functional requisites, was sound for its time. What they do not admit is that, in many ways, the program was better suited to its era than present programs are for today.

The two-year program devoted the first year to social knowledge of a general nature and a review of the entire field. At the end of this first year, students made their special vocational choices for the future. The second year was preparation for specialization. Courses were open to both men and women; the minimum age was 23 for full-time students, 20 for part-time students.

Requirements for all students included weekly classes in two main subject divisions: (a) state economy and sociology, state institutions, public health, and a review of the various problems which bear upon the social welfare subjects; and (b) welfare of the poor, direction of workers' housing, Toynbee work (settlement work), aid to deserted children, and overseeing in factories and workshops.

Practical training during the first year included optional attendance at cooking classes in a school of domestic science. Besides participation in lectures and conferences, students also visited social institutions and factories. The second-year program included participation in activities related to the vocational specialization of the student, under adequate supervision.

Even optional courses in cooking would horrify modern professionals, though there is little question some clients would benefit from help with cooking and straightening the house from today's friendly visitor. At a statewide social welfare conference in the 1960s, professionals were amazed that a volunteer, reluctantly given a hard-core case, had succeeded where therapeutic professionals had failed. The volunteer had rolled up her sleeves to help the client clean house, instead of writing process reports on the living conditions. The volunteer also had made soup for the children. Before long, the story reported, the house was in order, the harried mother quieted, the children returned to school, and the client began expressing some interest in avenues of change.

The Amsterdam program at the first school of social work stressed the need for a scientific perception of problems, leading to a general sociological understanding, as well as knowledge of a large field of legislation and an historical study of various problems. At the same time, the program emphatically stressed that the practical nature of the work necessitated active participation and experience in the daily task chosen in the field, carried out under adequate supervision that was scientific as well as inspiring.

Happily for those who appreciate realism, the search for the generic had not begun. It was wisely assumed that social workers brought special talents and inclinations to the helping field, and that these workers might be counted upon to exercise judicious choice in the field of their own choosing (United Nations, 1958, pp. 109–110).

C.O.S. School of Sociology

If the first C.O.S. School of Sociology, founded in 1903 and enjoying only a brief existence, maintained a separation from the larger academic community, nevertheless it did attempt a two-year integrated course of theory and practice and paid formal allegiance to the need for scientific knowledge. Professor Urwick, in his Introductory Lecture, said: " 'There is a new knowledge; in it may be found the scientific basis for the social education we need; and it is essential that the worker should learn it' " (United Nations, 1958, pp. 110–111).

The new knowledge was divided into: (1) the *natural history of society*—that which deals with how society and the individual grow and change; (2) what they can and ought to grow and change into, or *social philosophy;* (3) the framework of economic necessities, or *social economics;* and (4) knowledge of the mental processes on which development depends, or *individual* and *social psychology.*

Social workers have not yet found the new knowledge, though, like Professor Urwick, they believe it can be found. It is clear from the hierarchy of knowledge sought at the C.O.S. School of Sociology that social knowledge was put in first place—a first wisdom social workers were later to lose. Social workers were not to be

> "mere practitioners, leaving to others the task of understanding the theory on which their work is based." Therefore they "must learn to realize the slow growth that lies behind each present condition and fact; to see in the social structure, whole or part, of state or of institution, the expression of a vital meaning; to feel beneath the seemingly plastic relationships of social life the framework of economic necessities; and to find in each casual tendency and habit the effect of slowly changing mental processes. Not the training of the man of science but the scientific attitude must be theirs; that at least is necessary if experience is to be used aright. And is it unreasonable to believe that experience so guided will lead to a higher level of administration, a surer touch in dealing with what we call our 'social problems'; and above all a better conception and fulfilment of our recognized social duties?" (United Nations, 1958, p. 115)

In this official wisdom of the first C.O.S. School of Sociology, field work, notably, was to include "the study of normal industrial and social conditions" as well as casework, district work, organiza-

108

tion, and specific activities under an experienced person in some branch of charitable work that was not primarily relief work.

The Third International Survey on *Training for Social Work* rightly notes: "There is an astonishingly modern ring about these courses in the basic principle of social work, with emphasis on case work, group work and community organization, on scientific knowledge and on the means of translating this into practice" (United Nations, 1958, p. 115).

District work, for example, involved the study of industrial conditions, wage rates, housing, sanitation, poor laws, charitable agencies, churches, trade unions, friendly societies, and clubs. Organization included cooperating on sound principles with various other agencies, organizing meetings, thrift agencies, and dispensaries, and working with local government bodies.

New York School of Philanthropy

In 1904, the first university department of social science in England was established at the University of Liverpool, following a training scheme at the Victoria Settlement for Women, and inspired by Charles Loch, Eleanor Rathbone, and Elizabeth McAdam. In the same year, the New York School of Philanthropy secured funds to institute a one-year, full-time course for social workers.

The New York School of Philanthropy courses in 1904–1905 were largely in lecture form, conducted by individuals or lecture teams. The United Nations Survey (1958) notes: "The broad scope of the series is so impressive that it seems worthwhile to illustrate it by reproducing the outlines which appeared in the school catalogue of the period" (p. 112).

Seven broad areas of study were included in the course material: Survey of the Field; The State in Its Relation to Charity; Racial Traits in the Population, a Study in Sociology; Constructive Social Work; The Care of Needy Families in Their Homes; Child Helping Agencies; and Treatment of the Criminal, Reformatory Methods, Probation.

Each of these broad areas included from four to nine special subjects. Group C, *Racial Traits in the Population, a Study in Sociology*, encompassed: Immigration, The Social Meaning of Immigration, Italian Characteristics, The Characteristics of Jews Coming from Eastern Europe, The American Negro, The Negro in the City, Health and Morality, Economic Conditions, The Characteristics of Slavs, and a special course, The New Basis of Civilization: A Study in Economics.

Constructive Social Work included: Social Work in Large Cities, Social Aspects of Sanitary Work, The Tuberculosis Problem, The

Scope and Function of the Board of Health, Welfare Work in Factories and Stores, Social Tendencies of Modern Industrialism, The Boys' Club, The Modern Church as a Factor in Social Progress, and the Visiting Nurse as a Social Factor.

The section entitled *Treatment of the Criminal, Reformatory Methods, Probation* is especially interesting, in that it reflects a social work concern with corrections that social work later felt could not be fitted into its nondirective Freudian framework. Lectures were given on: The New Penology, Its Principles and Problems; Prison Labor; Minor Correctional Institutions; Principles and Methods of Reformatory Work; Probation Work for Girls and Women; and The Practical Art of Dealing with Wayward Girls.

Supervised field work consisted of casework under C.O.S. auspices and placements in an agency of the student's choice. Once a week, the student made excursions to other agencies.

There is much to be said for this older model of field work placement, as there is for the use of the concept "practical art." The modern school of social work often limits students' choice of placements for many reasons: lack of initiative in finding suitable placements; a disdain for other than "professional" placements, which, on occasion, has excluded such placements as juvenile and adult courts and their services; and the social work thesis that a student expressing too strong a preference for a particular placement is admitting some psychological defect, when he or she should be promising full and generic treatment capabilities in all situations, regardless of personality propensities.

In contrast to earlier flexibility, Schubert (1965) lists a series of present social work dilemmas that point up the repetitiveness of complaints about field work, dating from Bruno in 1944 and Hamilton in 1942.

> The question before us is this: How can we act wisely in management of the field course, how can we select a plan of action to guide present and future decisions, when we are confronted only with choices between unsatisfactory alternatives, problems seemingly incapable of satisfactory solutions? The one hopeful note here is the use of the word "seemingly"; some of our dilemmas, if studied carefully enough, may be transformed into problems that will yield to rational solutions. (p. 35)

Whatever the lack of sophistication in the early field work programs, there is no indication of a special attempt to measure student suffering in the process. In 1965, as Schubert notes, regardless of the school outline for evaluation of student process, "individual instructors vary in their emphasis on what the student is now able to do, how much he suffered while he was learning to do it, how much he grew, or how much potential for future development he shows" (p. 38).

In 1911, the one-year course at the New York School of Philanthropy was extended to two years, and the School became the New York School of Social Work.

The Chicago Institute

In Chicago, too, though early courses varied somewhat from year to year, "they were all related to social problems, which we would recognize today as concerns of social workers" (United Nations, 1958, p. 114).

In 1903, the same year as the founding of the C.O.S. School of Sociology in England, the Chicago Institute of Social Science was inaugurated by the Extension Division of the University of Chicago to offer training in social problems. This Institute became the Chicago School of Civics and Philanthropy in 1908, offering full-time training in social work under such leaders as Graham Taylor, Allen T. Burns, Edith Abbott, and Sophonisba Breckinridge.

In 1920, the Chicago School became the first in the United States to become affiliated with a university, as the Graduate School of Social Service Administration of the University of Chicago.

If these early courses in social work lacked some coherence, if they were largely descriptive, nevertheless there is evidence of "the conscious aim of distilling underlying principles from factual material and from practice . . . clearly apparent in the stated objectives of the courses" (United Nations, 1958, p. 114).

As Helen Wright notes, early leaders " 'recognized the necessity of preparing students to render the direct services for which people came to social agencies, to understand the findings of social research, and even to use research methods for the advancement of knowledge, and to participate in efforts to modify the social conditions inimical to the growth and development of the individual' " (United Nations, 1958, p. 114).

The Third International Survey concludes that "the pioneers in these 'under-developed' areas of Amsterdam, Chicago, London and New York discovered empirically what would be regarded at the present day as essentially the right answers about the subjects and methods of social work education. . . . All the same . . . they were only at the beginning of building up the content, evolving teaching methods, undertaking research and producing the necessary teaching material" (p. 118).

The Chicago School

As in the early days of the C.O.S., social work beginnings in America were marked by some crisscrossing of scientific and humanitarian impulses and personalities. Robert Faris (1967) writes that the early body of sociologists in the United States recruited numerous restless and dissatisfied clergymen. "The combination may account for the considerable pull of early sociology in the humanitarian direction and may also account for the not uncommon linking into one university department of sociology and professional training for social work" (p. 7).

In the 1920s, the period in which the Chicago School of Sociologists "held a sort of temporary performance championship in the United States, which in that time also meant the world leadership of sociology" (Faris, 1967, xiii), a Local Community Research Committee was established to stimulate interdepartmental studies on spatial patterns and forms of cultural life. Edith Abbott, head of the School of Social Service Administration, was among the first members of this committee, which also included Leon C. Marshall, head of the Department of Economics, Charles Merriam, head of the Political Science Department, Marcus Jernigan, Professor of History, and E. W. Burgess, Department of Sociology, coauthor of the famous textbook, *Introduction to the Science of Sociology* (1921).

When academic training in social work, once generally allied with sociology in a single department, withdrew into separate departments and schools, the result of the separation was "the chill that is characteristic of feelings between divorced couples" (Faris, 1967, p. 13).

As in England, the option of sociology was open to early social workers. In the United States, this option was represented by the group of assorted humanitarians and converts from other disciplines enthusiastically institutionalizing sociology in the rich interdisciplinary climate of the Chicago School. "It is partly a discovery of the Chicago urban research that the characteristic extremes of poverty, disease, and behavior troubles found everywhere in slum populations are products of social disorganization, rather than of low genetic quality in the populations" (Faris, 1967, p. 57). As in England, alternatives to the sociological approach included the 19th-century eugenics movement and its adherents, including biologists, a number of sociologists, and a good share of the general public.

The five-volume *The Polish Peasant in Europe and America*, by W. I. Thomas and Florian Znaniecki, originally published 1918–1921, was considered the most significant piece of research for peer discussion. "The handling of immigrants by social workers . . . is said to have been greatly altered in view of Thomas's notions concerning the phases of disorganization and reorganization experienced by the immigrants—a view far more sophisticated than the earlier conceptions attributing their troubles to biological inferiority" (Faris, 1967, pp. 18–19).

Why Was Wisdom Lost?

In Britain, the major reason advanced for the loss of that early wisdom is a divorce between theory and practice. "To analyse why this happened would not be profitable for the purpose of this study since it is already clear that essentially the wrong turning was a divorce between theory and practice. This took different forms as training for social work began to spread to other countries in the first part of the twentieth century" (United Nations, 1958, p. 118).

This divorce between theory and practice was responsible for the "comparatively narrow margin of difference in performance between the trained and the untrained" (p. 118), a narrow margin which became, to a social work defensively asserting its professional status, a major reason for excluding the untrained and paraprofessionals from its consideration.

Hope for present leadership is placed in American social work, which, according to the mystique of social work literature, continued along the lines of early integrated theory and practice, absorbing material from the social and behavioral sciences and struggling to apply this in practice, as well as feeding back observation from the field into the theoretical structure. Unfortunately, the evidence does not support this hope.

Present-day curricula of many of the older schools, as well as newer schools of Asia and Australia, are reported to be based on such interrelated theory and practice,

> while in other countries the world over great efforts are being made to heal the breach between theory and practice. Various attempts to test out and use generic principles of social work in different cultural settings are a significant development at the present day. Unfortunately they have so far gone almost unnoted from the point of view of systematic recording and study of the results. (United Nations, 1958, pp. 118–119)

It is not for the timid to suggest to social work "what objectives we should try to set for ourselves in the future"—the last element of Younghusband's invitation to assess social work's past. At least formally, social work claims to know what objectives are valid. What does *not* emerge from social work's past—and this is the conclusion of our analysis of the social work mystique—is that social work clearly and unambiguously understands the liability of this mystique in seeking future change.

A New Model

Besides gathering new allies, social work will have to move unambiguously toward the social sciences to build a respectable scientific theory. This clear movement certainly was not manifest when social work announced its coming of age in 1965, nor were there significant signs of such movement over the next five years.

It has been the author's experience that students prepared in a respectable sociology department on the A.B. level generally are overprepared for the social science content of the M.S.W. This may explain, in part, the finding by Aldridge and McGrath (Mossman, 1965) that there was very little relationship between the amount of work taken in undergraduate social sciences in general, and sociology in particular, and grades in graduate schools in social work.

This finding Mossman terms "surprising" in view of the stated support of graduate faculties for undergraduate strength in the social sciences, though Mossman finds "disturbing" the responses of most of the professional social work educators interviewed in the Aldridge and McGrath study, who "gave the impression of complacency and satisfaction with the pattern of social work education with little expressed interest in any variation. It is my belief that this is not true" (pp. 63–64).

As a point of fact, previous mastery of social science is not the real issue: deviancy is, and deviancy from accepted institutional values always leaves its mark on the grading system.

It is interesting to note the special social work methodology involved in the study reviewed by Mossman, who observes: "It was interesting that social science courses, other than sociology, completed with high grades were found better predictors of high grades in graduate school than high grades in undergraduate courses in sociology. One striking correlation ($+.876$) was that of the students who had taken in excess of fifteen hours of social welfare courses as undergraduates and had excellent graduate school records. However, since the number of students who fell in this category was so small (four), this finding suggests only that there is need for further study in this area" (p. 63).

At the 1964 Annual Program Meeting of the Council on Social Work Education, Sidney Berengarten reported on students enrolled in schools of social work in 1961–1962. The proportion of undergraduate majors in Social Welfare, English, Philosophy, and History who were rated superior by the social work schools was higher than the proportion of students who majored in Psychology or Sociology. The marginal and counseled-out rate was lowest for Social Welfare undergraduate majors and highest for social science majors (Stein, 1965, p. 63).

Stein suggests: "Whatever the reasons for the relatively poor showing of the Sociology and Psychology majors—and it would be well worth finding out the reasons—it seems clear that at least those undergraduate Social Welfare majors who are accepted tend to do quite well in graduate school.

"The question is whether we are doing well enough by them.

Even in the best schools, it is doubtful whether we are doing justice to our ablest students" (p. 64).

Apparently, the hypothesis that there is an especially strong connection between social welfare undergraduate courses and traditional social work graduate fare did not occur to Stein. Mossman (1965) seems equally innocent of cause-and-effect possibilities when he concludes his review of the Aldridge and McGrath study with the following questions:

> Why do students with undergraduate concentrations in the social sciences seem to have no advantages in graduate professional education over those who do not? Do students who major in social welfare have any advantages? What about the performance of these students in practice? As the study asks in conclusion: "Do the educational practices which social work educators see as desirable meet the needs of our contemporary society?" (pp. 64–65)

Even the results of random, representative sampling done with some sophistication probably will not convince social workers of the need for the social sciences so long as the strong bias against inclusion, tantamount to a fear of serious contamination, persists.

The Aldridge-McGrath study reported interviews with graduate deans, faculty, and students in schools of social work, which "reaffirm essentially the earlier study findings" (Mossman, 1965, p. 64).

There was agreement among those interviewed that professional social work should be graduate work, based on a broad liberal arts program in the humanities and the natural and social sciences.

There was no support for the idea of a continuum between undergraduate and graduate work, as recommended by the Curriculum Study of 1959. There was recognition of the drastic need for manpower and acknowledgment of the need for an undergraduate course or two in social welfare as part of liberal education, but opposition to any undergraduate offerings in social work, especially in methods and field experience. There also was opposition to an undergraduate social welfare major as desirable preparation for admission to graduate school or for beginning employment, a most unusual finding in view of the success of social welfare undergraduate majors in graduate social work (Mossman, 1965, p. 64).

The near end of the journey into social work's past and its problems is not too different from its beginnings: a seemingly inexhaustible reservoir of optimistic resolutions promising a future destined to bring about the millennium of integrated theory and practice.

NEW MODELS AND ALLIES

To the extent that one sees the process of professional social work education as a break with the student's academic past and identity as total and drastic as that of a "carpenter being re-educated to become a watchmaker" (E. Walsh, 1965, pp. 49–50), the necessary professional options of the 1970s have not been understood. Social work's Topsy, who, as Younghusband concedes, never has been a model of child nurture, remains analogously at the professional "magician" stage, midway between two worlds, absorbed by magic thinking, the earliest mental activity accompanying the need satisfaction principle of early development (Fraiberg, 1959, Chapter 4).

Similarly, to the degree that social work educators speak of "more readiness to risk the students' exposure to divergent points of view" (Kadushin, 1965, p. 39), the import of past historical choices has been underestimated.

So ends the journey into social work's past through its literature. Despite proclamations of maturity, the social work profession's child remains at a preverbal, egocentric stage of scientific thought.

Wootton may well be correct that social workers, happily, do better than they write. There still remain the problems of explaining a "coming of age" with the admitted loss of many client groups—including social work's historic client, the poor—and assessing the current list of endless dilemmas and unresolved questions.

There is no doubt that historical choices have had a profound effect on the work social workers do; on the value system the profession, or semi-profession, espouses; and on the officially sanctioned socializing atmosphere, in classroom and field. Social workers and their critics alike agree that a new model of helping is needed if social work is to become the hospitable university center for practical application of scientific principles—the key to the vision for 1990 presented in 1966 by former Secretary of Health, Education, and Welfare, John W. Gardner.

Mark P. Hale (1966) outlines a traditional model in use for 90% of students enrolled in schools of social work in 1964: " 'Treatment oriented practice' is the main focus in the curriculum, with knowledge, attitude, and skills related more to treatment than to the emerging wider professional role articulated by the 1962 Curriculum Policy Statement" (p. 37). Traditionally, two-thirds of the student's organized time is spent in the field, where the field instructor is the key person in the student's learning experience, "often . . . mentor, role model, teacher, master, curriculum developer, counselor, supervisor, therapist, and authority figure" (p. 36).

Hale sees stress in this model, despite wide support among educators, and suggests "a need for considerable experimentation and innovation in social work education if an educational plan viable for the future in relation to all the parameters is to be produced" (p. 38).

In 1965, Samuel Finestone concluded that research in social work education "would be advanced" if answers could be found to the following questions: (1) What is an appropriate way of viewing social work education as a whole? (2) What research questions are generated by this comprehensive overview, and what classification scheme usefully orders them? (3) What are the results of categorizing existing research according to this classification? Which categories are adequately represented by existing research, and where are the gaps? (4) What priorities for the program of research are suggested by considering the gaps and their relative importance? (5) How can the research program be implemented (p. 18)?

Finestone's model, offered with the disclaimer that no single definitive construct of so complex a phenomenon as social work can suffice, consists of a series of circles, indicating that social work receives recruitment input and produces graduate output. The educational program of a school of social work is shown related to a graduate school in an unspecified interaction, to undergraduate schools and social agencies, to field work programs in the practice area, and to manpower utilization on the output side.

Social work's relationship to the vital institutions of the community is designated simply as *community*. The model indicates that social work schools have administrators, faculty, students, and a physical structure, as well as dropouts in the application, selection, or educational processes. It also indicates that schools of social work have relationships with the Council on Social Work Education and the National Association of Social Workers (p. 20).

Scientific Army

It is fair to conclude that, as of 1969, some 100 years after C.O.S. Secretary Loch called for a growing army of increasingly well-trained social workers, the official literature does not give assurance that Loch's hope has been fulfilled. The year 1969 is used advisedly. In conversation, social workers claim that new insights are being garnered, and new, exciting projects are being undertaken. As this is the ubiquitous promise of the official literature, we must look to the most recent literature, since 1969, for evidence of that progress.

There are two broad results of social work's historical options, results which reinforce each other. Intellectually, explanation of past choices and their consequences has produced a mystique of optimism. To maintain that mystique, in turn, the socializing atmosphere for graduate level students has calcified into a markedly rigid official posture. What should have developed into a pliable, graceful, open art form since Loch instead has represented itself with the assurance of pure scientific principles, with severe penalties for deviation by the unbelieving. Edith Abbott's assessment over 40 years ago remains appropriate: It is "in part because our field has been neglected by the scholar that progress has often been lamentably slow" (1931, p. 2).

Abbott approved Arnold Toynbee's evaluation that "to make benevolence scientific is the great problem of the present day." Those who are convinced that we put into practice even less than we know would concede that social work's future direction will have a significant bearing on any marriage between theory and practice in the broader social helping area.

Vocational Incest

Gilbert Geis (1965) is on sure ground when he concludes that accurate predictions cannot be made for all vocational pursuits, and that in social work specifically there remains considerable uncertainty regarding the most effective means and personnel needed to achieve the goals of the profession.

> In the absence of standards, the tendency is to assume that what is currently being done by leaders in the field represents the best method and that these people represent an inventory of attributes requisite for the most satisfactory performance. Yet, if people are advised to follow careers in social work on the grounds that their qualifications resemble those of the establishment, this can lead only to vocational incest. (p. 27)

Such a method, Geis suggests, may deprive the field of individuals who, by virtue of their very differentness, may be the ones to resolve some of the pressing issues facing modern social work.

The nature and extent of differentness that social work can absorb and tolerate is, when all has been said and restated, the crucial issue. Indeed, social work is not unique in the necessity to reexamine principles and process to meet new needs.

The context within which basic policy decisions are made, says Margaret S. Schubert, Ph.D., "is that of a conflict of values between the practice world and the academic world, a conflict apparent since the days of apprenticeship." This conflict exists not only between agency-employed practitioners and university-employed classroom teachers, "it colors communication among classroom teachers as well" (1965, p. 40).

If there is no question that historical choices have had consequences, there is no question that social workers themselves have been critical of certain aspects of these choices. The ambiguity results from social work's long tradition that practice is more important to the social worker than knowledge, and that whatever knowledge is required is best obtained from social workers themselves, engaging in continuous mining of the profession's practice principles and suppositions.

Considering the magnitude of social problems and the lack of an integrated social science framework, considerable sympathy may be mustered for Bertram Beck's complaint that social workers do not need anyone telling them to change but do need help in adaptation. In fairness to the task social workers face, it must be admitted that the profession's two ubiquitous problems, scientific adaptation and realignment with the social, are equally society's problems. To a great extent, the tensions between ameliorism and social structural change which social work faced at its beginnings persist today in American society.

The Present Option

The following discussion, rather than proposing a new social work model, will focus on an overall social work atmosphere in which such a model may be constructed by social workers themselves. Two broad aspects are involved: (1) utilization of social work allies; and (2) the insertion of a partial framework from sociology in the area of deviancy, as an example of a more realistic approach than certain of social work's previous preoccupations in that area. These considerations flow naturally from certain broad conclusions about the merits of social work's previous choices: (1) that social work, to be a valid helping institution, must provide an atmosphere open to insights from the previous academic and life experiences of students and faculty, from social movements within the community, and from the evolving social consensus of the larger society; and (2) that social work must borrow from the sciences, especially the social sciences.

Social Work Allies

Some allies are readily available to social workers.

Speaking to social workers in 1963 on the larger question of a social welfare position, Dr. William H. Form, Professor, Department of Sociology and Anthropology, Michigan State University, called for political socialization of social workers to achieve a new professional posture in centrally planned change. Form proposed two requisites: (1) convincing the main groups in welfare that power conflict not be continued along traditional lines and that the developmental model of planning be tried; and (2) perhaps more important, abandoning inappropriate perspectives of power to accommodate the shift in the conception of American society and the nature of change within it.

> Difficult as the adoption of this new perspective may be for other groups, social workers may find it more stressful to abandon their present neutral professional posture. If my conception of the character of social workers is accurate, this change will be stressful because the profession tends to breed a type that is timid, conservative, unimaginative, and easily co-opted by the tough-minded. (Form, 1964, pp. 88–89)

The explicitly neutral pose, adopted as the "professional way" of behaving, more likely than not leads to legitimate welfare claims being preempted by local conservative interests. Such a professional administrative style, as W. Joseph Heffernan, Jr., described it in a 1964 paper on social work executives, involves pushing a program by working privately through professional organizations, agency boards, and powerful people, avoiding identification with a political party and with interests such as organized labor, an ally of social welfare.

Such a professional style, Form concludes, has resulted in the fact that rarely in American history has so little influence been wielded by a major group as that recorded by professional welfare administrators:

> Although immersed in a political context and afraid to take a stand on controversial issues, the professional welfare administrator wants to broaden welfare services, re-organize existing services, and rationally plan and centrally direct new welfare programs. On the surface, these would appear to be unrealistic goals for such politically naive people. As a matter of fact, rarely in American history has so little influence been wielded by a group that has had so much opportunity to influence. Although the clientele of social work is enormous, it has never been organized to back expanded welfare programs. While it is true that the clientele has been underprivileged, underpoliticized, dependent, and of low status, it has on occasion been organized successfully by educators, politicians, labor unions, and other pressure groups. (p. 87)

It should be mentioned here that even on so fundamental a violation of public welfare recipients' rights as the midnight raid, social workers waited a year after a lawyer called attention to violations of the Fourth and Fourteenth Amendments to the Constitution before reacting. Charles Reich, Assistant Professor of Law at Yale

University, published a study, "Midnight Welfare Searches and the Social Security Act," in 1963. In a second article, published in 1964, Reich further explored the implications of surprise visits made to the homes of welfare recipients either on Sunday mornings or after midnight. In 1964, the National Association of Social Workers "protested vigorously against the violation of the civil rights of welfare recipients and has condemned the unethical implications of 'midnight raids' " (Titmuss, 1965, pp. 73–74).

Even without organized social work's political influence, says Form, the growth of welfare institutions in the United States proceeded primarily as a response by government to the recognition that existing mechanisms could not solve society's problems. Once legislation had been enacted and bureaucracies organized, professional social workers and social work schools validated and legitimated these social forms. With no unified power structure to force the growth of the welfare sector in the past and no unified coalition to halt its growth and diffusion in the present, however, there is an inevitable "institutionalization of welfare programs that are overlapping, inefficient, unimaginative, unintegrated, tardy, and sometimes damaging to the people they intend to serve." To meet growing welfare needs, this welfare sector, Form points out, must be able to move rapidly to institute rationally developed programs with less restraint, and receive greater public recognition in the process. "This is what I take to be the task of centrally planned change" (p. 87).

Obviously, says Form, the new professional posture of social work cannot take place without support from others and without changes in current social work training. In a retraining of social workers, social science itself is at stake in the effort to use acquired knowledge to meet the problems of a changing social world. To this end, all of the social sciences must become allies of social work, both in training social workers and in helping them to institute programs. Basic social sciences also must test their theories and knowledge in the marketplace of social action, as the applied disciplines abandon their disesteemed and isolated niches in the universities.

For social work itself, Form concludes:

At the risk of alienating everybody and displaying my own biases, I suggest that social work de-emphasize its clinical bias, its overemphasis on casework and group work, and come back home to the social sciences. I realize that social work has been undergoing agonizing self-analysis of its training programs as evidenced by the recent volumes of the Curriculum Study [1959, 13 volumes]. I do not believe that the recommendations proposed there are tough enough. Social welfare students need even more training in political science, social organization, administrative theory, social stratification, social psychology, and so on. (p. 89)

To this end, Form feels, the university itself can no longer toler-

122

ate the artificial distinction between the pure and applied sciences, just as the larger community can no longer tolerate the barriers of communication between people of science and people of action.

Preoccupation with the Particular

Speaking at an international conference of schools of social work in 1964, Richard Titmuss, of the London School of Economics and Political Science, University of London, explicated the problem:

> At the heart of the paradox is the infrequency with which we in schools of social work venture out into such academically hazardous waters in our workaday lives. We do not discuss social research, social policy, and the role of schools of social work in abstract, universal terms. When we discuss such subjects at all—which is seldom enough—we do so within concrete, specific frameworks. We talk about peoples' feelings, or their facial responses in the casework relationship, but always in reference to particular clients or client groups. When we discuss social policy we do so in terms of particular, definite problems. . . . When we discuss research—which today, like science, is a word to be uttered in terms of hushed reverence—we have in mind specific, small, and tangible projects. In our daily round of activities with students, colleagues, clients, and agencies we tend to restrict ourselves to the immediate, the intimate, the precise, and the manageable. (1965, p. 68)

The public mood, though neither homogeneous nor infallible, is not marked by such arch timidity. With or without social work, organization will take place. It is only practical to recognize the differences that mark the present-day "client," and to use these differences in a new, positive alliance.

The New Client

The discussion at the International Council of Social Work Education seminar, held in cooperation with the East-West Center at the University of Hawaii in February 1966, does not reflect the drastic shifts in self-concept and expectations of social work's new client. Reporting on the event, Dame Eileen Younghusband (1966) noted:

> The "cliché" that casework is a luxury was examined. It was obvious that it can be afforded to only a limited extent and in developing countries only in particular places, and that there are many higher priorities and more appropriate services in such countries. For example, it is absurd to use trained caseworkers to interview public assistance applicants in dire poverty and primarily in need of food, clothing, and shelter. In other circumstances, it may not be the casework method but the service that is inappropriate, as in starting a child guidance clinic before basic child welfare services exist. (p. 64)

The client that social work discussed at this international seminar no longer exists, if he or she ever did. "The term 'client' took some hard knocks. This was partly because in community work, frequently it is not possible to decide who *is* the client, and partly because the term implies a contract to serve a particular individual or group, whereas it is becoming increasingly clear that the appropriate function of social work lies in intervention in a system rather than commitment to a given client. . . . The 'client' is thus not a person but a variable in a process" (Younghusband, 1966, p. 63).

The deserving poor of early Charity Organisation Society ministrations have turned into a variable in a process as social work moves toward the language of the social sciences. If casework, even assuming that its concepts and techniques are revised drastically, is a "luxury" because "it is absurd to use trained caseworkers to interview public assistance applicants in dire poverty and primarily in need of food, clothing, and shelter," the casework approach most certainly will be misapplied to a variable in a process.

The Volunteer As Ally

By its consistent disregard of the resources of the volunteer, social work has failed to utilize still another aspect of that broad public which presumably has been the profession's concern.

Few aspects of social work during this century, writes Samuel Mencher, have been the source of as much concern and controversy as the organization and function of voluntary social service. This discussion has been associated with two major developments of the 20th century: the rise of governmental responsibility for social welfare and the growth of social work as a profession.

Discussion has focused primarily on those problems arising out of immediate needs and conflicts, rather than on the formulation of fundamental issues. Voluntaryism, however, says Mencher (1959), cannot be viewed solely in relation to the assumption of governmental responsibility or social work professionalism. "For voluntary activity, its nature and scope, broadly affects the structure of society and the relationship of its members to each other and to society as a whole" (p. 219).

Protecting its deep need to establish its own professionalism, which Mencher identifies with the rise of the Charity Organisation movement and the beginnings of scientific casework in the last two decades of the 19th century, modern American social work has not made imaginative use of the volunteer since that time, despite Mary Richmond's 1905 warning:

> During this last decade more especially, our national habit of thought has exalted the expert and the professional at the expense of the volunteer. By those who hold the extreme of this view, it is assumed that only officials should be permitted to be charitable. (Richmond, 1930, p. 220; quoted in Mencher, 1959, p. 222)

The volunteer has not quite met social work's self-definition, which began to emerge early in the separation of voluntary and professional roles by the C.O.S. Assistance became solely the responsibility of the paid worker. Mary Richmond's misgivings have come home to roost:

> Against a certain opinionated and self-righteous attitude in some of the trained social workers themselves we have to be especially on our guard. This world is not a stage upon which we professional workers are to exercise our talents, while the volunteers do nothing but furnish the gate-receipts and an open-mouthed admiration of our performances. (Richmond, 1930, p. 345; quoted in Mencher, 1959, p. 227)

By 1965, Stein concluded: "There is little new to say about the problem of a respectable career line for the untrained worker other than there should be one" (p. 61). That same year, the National Association of Social Workers considered the issue of whether schools of social work can and should cooperate by helping agencies on a consultative basis to set up staff development programs, using their own facilities for occasional lectures, special institutes, or summer programs. In actual fact, however, modern social work's accommodation of the volunteer was no better in 1965 than when Mary Richmond warned of self-righteousness.

Stein proceeded to foretell the multitude of problems that social work's cooperation with the volunteer would entail:

> It takes staff and energy in scarce supply away from its own programs and weakens the agency's opportunity to develop its own training capacity, modeled to its own needs. Moreover, graduate school faculties are not equipped, by and large, to give short-term training to do specific jobs. They are presumably educators concerned with broad skills, not trainers to induct people into the particular tasks of particular agencies. (p. 61)

If, as Kadushin asserted that same year, the social work program on the Master's level was not graduate education either in content or level, the caveat about dilution of principles by the volunteer suggests a lack of imagination.

Stein asks that the difference between education and training be kept clear. When schools engage in in-service training to the extent of controlling it, he says, they are apt to distort what should be rapid and scientific preparation into a generalized pocket edition of broad professional education. "This error is compounded by agency administrators who in all good faith and conscience turn to the schools to bail them out when they hire totally unprepared people" (p. 61).

Social work's professional horror story of that year concerned one such group, which asked a graduate school of social work to permit recent college graduates, presumably undergoing in-service training for group work in poverty areas, to take a few courses, such as normal and abnormal personality and behavior.

Presenting such courses out of context to raw job recruits and calling it in-service training is one of the surest ways of creating profound and long-lasting confusion. Graduate schools should stand ready to use their resources to enable agencies to conduct more effective staff development programs and to help them experiment with new techniques and content. (Stein, 1965, p. 61)

As early as 1915, Edith Abbott, then Associate Director of the Chicago School of Civics and Philanthropy, urged staff instructors to raise the standards of social work being done in all areas of the country, because the "greatest handicap is . . . the need of trained workers. It is precisely this handicap that is our own and only excuse for being" (p. 621).

The early wisdom on the necessity of service in the creation of the good society apparently was lost, too, with professionalization. On this utilization of the potential of the volunteer, Mencher (1959) notes that the British seem to have made a better adjustment in supplementing public programs with voluntary bodies. "On the whole, British nongovernmental organizations conform more closely to 'voluntary' than to 'private' effort. Professionalism and bureaucracy have not made the same impress as on the American scene" (p. 236, n. 27). Woodroofe (1962) makes a similar observation: "for despite a greater readiness to recognize its worth and to use its services, social work in Great Britain is less 'professionalized' than in the United States" (p. 214).

By moving away from the clinical and the psychiatric, social work should be able to face its client neither as a variable in an intervention system nor as a mindless being incapable of understanding his or her own problems. The latter view, the result of a too heavy reliance on Freudianism, has been described by Woodroofe:

Sometimes, of course, the caseworker was carried away by her self-imposed mission to explore the subconscious. Often she had drunk so deeply of Freudian draughts that she claimed to know more about the client than he knew himself; or else she insisted upon taking the hard way out, refused to accept at face value the emergencies which propelled many people to seek the aid of an agency, and sought to penetrate below what she called "the presenting problem" to the "something deeper" that was assumed to lie beneath. (p. 131)

The Ally of Religion

Freudian "listening with the third ear" has been applied also to clients presenting problems of religious significance. These problems often were dismissed as manifestations of a client's concern with another problem—usually one of the social worker's own making (Hartman, 1962).

In the total reality situation, religious values and motivations play a significant role. Protest movements of minority groups have been strongly religious in character. It is ironic that social work, despite its claim to a link with the heritage of great religious social reformers, should have dismissed peremptorily the religious presenting problems of clients. A continuation of this attitude will deprive social work of ready allies in religious movements.

In his doctoral study, Charles Hartman (1962) found that "a positive regard for religion in the caseworkers' own philosophical framework did not determine their handling of religious issues in practice. . . .

"Half of the caseworkers interviewed stated that they would focus on the apparently unmet psychological or social needs, which, in the opinion of the caseworkers, were expressed in the defense of religion" (p. 3).

It is significant, of course, that the official discussion of values does not embrace explicitly support of the client's faith.

Since social work has been allied with psychiatry for more than 50 years, pretensions of members of the profession to being junior psychiatrists will be relinquished only grudgingly. If social work does not examine critically its psychiatric grounding, however, it will be unable to examine critically the merits of alternative approaches which have been reaching the general public.

If social work's old clientele, the deserving poor, no longer are grateful or even willing to be judged deserving, social work's second historical clientele, those judged to need psychiatric counseling, are remarkably more knowledgeable about current developments than is social work's own official literature.

New works on personal coping have proliferated geometrically, and social work should have been busy in the 1960s dealing with the implications for its traditional psychiatric approach of books already stocked on popular bookshelves: William Glasser, M.D., *Reality Therapy: A New Approach to Psychiatry*, 1965; Thomas S. Szasz, M.D., *The Myth of Mental Illness: Foundations of a Theory of Personal Conduct*, 1961; Eric Berne, M.D., *Games People Play: The Psychology of Human Relationships*, 1964; Thomas A. Harris, M.D., *I'm OK— You're OK: A Practical Guide to Transactional Analysis*, 1967. The profession should be officially and practically more alert to new possibilities than the client.

Social Work's Faculty

Another social work ally is the social work faculty itself. As late as 1965, social work set itself to determining the attributes of a successful social work educator.

Two working papers presented at the Thirteenth Annual Program Meeting of the Council on Social Work Education addressed themselves to this "very complex process." Ruth Smalley pleaded for " 'an "interesting" self in lively possession of its own uniqueness as an individual.' " Maurice Connery spoke of " ' "identity" as an attribute, stressing that a successful social work educator must first achieve and maintain his identity as a social worker' " (Blackey, 1965, p. 6). The emphasis was heavily clinical. The educators agreed that prerequisite to any of these requirements was a knowledge of one's own and related fields, but even this was inconclusive. "The criteria for judging and measuring the qualification in a prospective candidate are still inadequately developed" (p. 8). The field does not have sufficient answers "to plot a course."

Significantly, after conceding that the basic core content of social work still has not been identified, although "it must certainly include familiarity with current learning theory and a working competence with the . . . 'structure' of a subject" (Blackey, 1965, p. 8), the group proposed a tutorial plan for new faculty members, as representing the second and third stages of learning. The tutorial plan would include orienting the new faculty member to the school's program, to the university community and the social work community of which the school is a part, and to his or her particular teaching assignments and work load.

In this tutorial plan, the new faculty member would be associated in a learning role with a senior colleague, in the same field where possible. Such a plan "should provide opportunities for the new faculty member to 'sit in' on courses taught by others on the faculty in order to get a sense of the curriculum as a whole, to plan and teach his own courses in close consultation with his tutorial advisor, and to participate in committee work on curriculum development and other aspects of the educational program. However, the new recruit must be allowed sufficient time to absorb and integrate what he is learning" (p. 11).

To propose a close tutorial plan for incoming social work faculty newly possessed of Master's or Doctorate degrees, and possibly new ideas, is to perpetuate social work's reliance on a tradition admittedly without a basic core content. The closely supervised field instruction of students has not been without hazards to creativity. Extending the plan to faculty members serves to restrict even further an already circumscribed role of younger faculty in contributing to social work's new model or models.

Student Allies

Complaints by students about the nature of social work classes and programs already have been discussed. In principle, students could become powerful allies of social work's highest aspirations. In my experience, however, student dissent has been viewed as a type of heresy, to be exorcised by stern suggestions to enter psychoanalysis.

Several such cases of misdiagnosis come readily to mind. One student who entered social work to become a community organizer was viewed as "sick" because he expressed disagreement with the determination of casework instructors to make him, in his words, a "junior psychiatrist." This evaluation was not made by qualified psychiatric personnel. As a penalty for protest, the student was asked to leave the school for a year to work in the community before seeking readmission—a novel way of handling school "failures" by foisting them on the community. There were enough instances of maladaptive handling of students who would have been considered assets in the normal academic situation to inspire in the observer fear for the hapless client. Some of the bowdlerized Freudian analysis done on students by M.S.W. instructors makes humorous small talk, but the consequences for student potential are serious indeed.

The argument that social work requires more than academic excellence, thus necessitating this constant temperature-taking of students' emotions, is not sufficient excuse. Criteria for judging nonacademic performance contain the same vagaries as do those which social workers, in moments of candor, admit have not worked for the client.

M.S.W.-qualified personnel apparently see no professional ethical breach in pontificating on student psyches for reports that will follow the students in later years. Moreover, this psychiatrically tinged atmosphere serves to divert student attention from problems that need attention. Informing a client that an agency charges fees becomes a monumental exercise in student self-examination. Expression of normal anxiousness about a client's problem by an unwary student, lulled by a sympathetic casework supervisor, becomes the subject of administrative probing and tugging. The expected consequences of thrusting a rural student upon urban clients, relatively sophisticated in the process of the welfare system, apparently are lost on educators.

Constant analysis of both faculty and student emotions and commitment to the supreme task of being a social worker, often wildly missing the reality mark, create an educational learning experience light-years removed from the best in the academic community. Students' candid autobiographical entry statements can become self-indictments on which the zealous practice their techniques for inducing emotional and attitudinal changes.

When faculty members and administrators dispense psychiatric evaluations of students and faculty alike, without adequate scientific precautions, they are, in a sense, practicing witchcraft without license. The academic community has some responsibility to urge candidates for helping roles to carefully screen their first impulse to tell all, in the same spirit as the *Gault* case in 1967 gave juveniles the right to protect themselves against self-incrimination.

William Schofield's *Psychotherapy: The Purchase of Friendship* (1964) makes the point well:

> Correction of this burgeoning socio-individual psychopathology demands action along two fronts: we must, at the same time, increase the number of persons who are adequately skilled and appropriately competent to converse therapeutically with the multitudes of the miserable and *also* effectively reduce the demand and need of such professional friendship. . . .
>
> We must honestly confront our citizens with those considerations which will encourage an intelligently humane social climate, a logistically reasonable structure of social services, and a restored respect for *individual* responsibility in that philosophical venture in which rests every person's greatest freedom—that searching of the unknown which is the essence of human life. (p. 3)

Social work students deserve as much. Trusting students' intelligence and good sense in applied areas has further implications for a new social work model. In experience with students on both the graduate and undergraduate levels, I remain convinced that they do not need—nor will they accept—constant monitoring of their view of reality. I am thinking especially of some very successful results of student growth in internships offered by academic institutions in applied areas. If students need good academic instruction and sometimes benefit from the previous experience of their elders, they generally are quite able to bring their own experience to bear in situational adaptation. Despite the catalogued and awesome responsibilities deemed inherent in field work programs, I remain in favor of less rather than more hand-holding.

The Private Practitioner

The social worker who dares to become a private practitioner has fared no better than client, student, and faculty in winning institutional social work's trust and escaping its censure. Moving against the historical norm that social work is practiced within a social work agency, some caseworkers have "gone into private practice." In doing so, they have become "deviants."

"The attitude toward private practice by caseworkers has been generally adverse. The prevailing attitude prior to 1955, as perceived by caseworkers both in and out of private practice, was that private practice was outside the definition of social work. The only published statements by leaders in social work education were negative. The institution reacted in the usual bureaucratic way of imputing 'dishonesty' to the motives of the deviant" (Levenstein, 1964, pp. 5–6).

Who Is the Social Worker?

The question of who or what a social worker is has not been solved to any real degree of satisfaction, but the discussion offers some clues for a future resolution.

In a 1959 paper on "The Professional Identity in Social Work," Norman A. Polansky offers two personality tendencies for which social work as an occupation may offer opportunities: a chance for sublimation and an ego-supportive job that helps in binding anxiety. "Both tendencies may contribute toward a kind of work in which one dedicates himself to helping others through a relationship" (p. 301).

"The first of these," Polansky writes, "which is fairly prevalent in the personalities of many of us in the helping professions, might as well be blatantly called 'oral-dependency striving.' This is the need to be loved, let us say, or be given to. Social workers as a group exhibit a vast amount of it. We eat, and we discuss food, we drink, and we discuss drinks; we smoke heavily. Whether we show more of this characteristic than some other occupational groups (e.g., nurses or dieticians), I do not know. As a matter of fact, the available statistics would be irrelevant in any case" (pp. 301–302).

Having raised the question of whether social workers as a group have a special need to be loved, Polansky's conclusion that statistics showing that social workers exhibit more or less oral-dependency striving are irrelevant is perplexing. Farmers may very well eat more than social workers, as may other groups within the population.

What does seem clear in Polansky's analysis is that the flight from hard data is a flight from the present reality situation. "If one assumes," says Polansky, "that oral dependency is a strong tendency among social workers, one can explain a number of problems for which 'social science theories' offer far less parsimonious hypotheses" (p. 302).

Common sense might offer the most parsimonious suggestion of all: namely, that people with a strong need to be loved ought not be counted upon to sublimate this need sufficiently to be entrusted with helping others. Regardless, the faith of American social work's British cousin in the professionalization and expertise on this side of the Atlantic does not seem merited by the literature. Rather, it appears to be precisely this American mis-emphasis on the professional, in contrast to Clare Winnicott's notion of the "social servant," that hampers creative new adjustment to a new image.

Winnicott, in an article on "Casework and Agency Function" (1962), suggests replacing the term *social worker* with *social servant*. The lowly status implied by the term *servant* will not make Winnicott's suggestion appealing to American social workers. Indeed, Max Siporin (1965) notes: "The image of the social worker as a dedicated social servant, which is projected by Mr. Timms and Mrs. Winnicott, is in marked contrast to the image of the professional practitioner delineated in this country" (p. 81).

Social Servant

The notion of social servant, however, whether or not that precise term is used, would have the effect of turning American social work's gaze outward, away from itself, toward areas of recognized functional need. It also would reduce the compulsion to use powerful socialization sanctions to ensure conformity to an empty professionalism.

In the meantime, the arithmetic of chronic manpower shortages shows an ever-widening gap between social work vacancies, especially in public service, and current supply. In the late 1960s, deans of nine New York schools of social work proposed a five-point plan for meeting this "chronic crisis."

With the graduate schools of New York operating at full capacity, three out of every four applicants were being turned away for lack of room. At the same time, there were approximately 4,700 vacancies, mostly in public agencies, requiring M.S.W. applicants. "If every M.S.W. worker went into public agencies (and they don't) it would take about eight graduating classes from all the schools merely to fill the vacancies—if the demand for social workers stood still" (pamphlet, Social Work Recruiting Center, New York).

The nine deans expressed commitment to a frontal attack on the manpower crisis and asked for the help of all concerned citizens—businessmen and civic groups, labor and the professions, voters and legislators—all social work's available allies.

In response to such a prestigious invitation, it seems fitting to conclude the journey into Topsy's social-land with a few suggestions regarding borrowing by social work from the field of sociology.

BACK HOME—TO THE SOCIAL SCIENCES

In the discussion of available social work allies, it was assumed that a process approach to borrowing would reemphasize social work's position as an ideal helping art—graceful, flexible, and generous in its concern for client and community, rather than jealous of professional image.

In the following discussion of borrowing from the social sciences in the building of a respectable theoretical framework, another assumption is made: that the best resource persons are those who are both trained in a particular science and sympathetic to the needs of the applied areas. It will not serve Form's invitation to social workers to go back home to the social sciences if the return is envisioned as encouraging them to pick and choose concepts that appear to be congruent with the social work tradition.

The fact that social workers have clung to conclusions of borrowed knowledge, such as material on maternal deprivation by Bowlby and Spitz, longer than the lending disciplines, which have subjected the studies to further research and analysis (Kadushin, 1959, p. 68), is good reason for letting representatives of lending disciplines teach their own subject matter.

Science—Not Savior

In considering the potential contribution of sociology to the new social worker of the 1970s, I have been warned by several social workers that the profession would not look kindly upon sociology being painted as its "savior." It bears repeating, therefore, that sociologists have too many problems of their own to undertake a task so momentous. It seems equally clear that not all material from sociology, or the other social sciences, will be useful to social workers. Social workers will need patience in converting the material of the social sciences to their action needs. They will need to be patient, too, with critics, who often are allies.

Training for Social Work: Third International Survey (United Nations, 1958), in reviewing previous findings of meetings convened by the United Nations on training for social work, observed that the "major emphasis" in the seminars was on the "extreme importance" of developing the teaching of relevant aspects of sociology and anthropology. There was general recognition that social workers must be knowledgeable about structure and function, and about the effects of cultural and subcultural patterns and values on behavior, motivation, and attitudes. There was agreement that considerable work remained to be done, both in teaching this subject matter in schools of social work and in translating knowledge from the social sciences into social work practice. Such knowledge was seen as essential for practitioners, social administrators, social planners, and policymakers (pp. 10–11).

Lady Barbara Wootton in 1967 noted a "significant change of attitude" in modern social workers since her own 1959 strictures. Her later remarks are worth repeating, inasmuch as they summarize a past social work philosophy largely at odds with reality and propose a solution—one that may not be palatable to a group of her colleagues, but which remains as much an option in the United States today as it was in England in the early years of the Charity Organisation Society.

Lady Wootton (1967) recalls some of her earlier criticisms of social work—in particular, "the appallingly arrogant image of themselves that social workers, largely under the influence of the American cult of psycho-analysis, have been at pains to present." Not surprisingly, she writes, her observations earned her a good deal of odium, although she had been careful to say "(what was generally overlooked) that the admirable work that social workers do bears no relation to the silly things that they are apt to say."

> What, however, nobody apparently appreciated was that my protest against the condescending attitudes portrayed in the literature of social work and against social workers' conviction of their own superior understanding of those whom they are pleased to call "their clients" and of their ability to discern "something deeper" underneath a simple request for practical help—what nobody seems to have appreciated is that my resentment of all this springs directly from my equalitarian philosophy. Just as the Lady Bountiful of an earlier generation dispensed material prosperity, so the social workers of to-day (or perhaps it is fairer to say of yesterday, for there has been a significant change of attitude) like to picture themselves as dispensing superior psychological insight. Each of these attitudes, in its own idiom, serves to underline the inferior status of the lower social classes to whom the social workers' services are mainly directed; and to me it has always been an astonishment that so many even of my socialist friends fail to recognize old style charitable assistance in its modern garb of "family casework." (p. 189)

Alternatives to Bolshevism

As Abrams notes in tracing sociology's beginnings in England, the science of Auguste Comte finally came to be seen by some as an alternative to Bolshevism, even as the Charity Organisation Society's casework, much later in the 20th century, still was seen by its followers as an alternative to the same Bolshevism. If the followers of Comte and the method ameliorists of the C.O.S. did not consider themselves as natural allies, at least some of the present confusion in applied areas may be understood as a result of the break between them in the search for solutions to the same modern problems of industrialization and urbanization.

The wisdom of particular political assessments—Lady Wootton's, the Comtean societies', or even Charles Booth's proposed individualism in the arms of socialism (the conclusion to a work firmly anchored in the sociological tradition)—is not at issue here. What is at issue in tracing social work's past options is its almost totally individualist response to problems that have cried for social structural solutions. The analyses of the social sciences, however inadequate, were necessary to the task: the social sciences were necessary allies.

Sociologists, or other social scientists, need not be warned again that social work will not look kindly upon designations of particular disciplines as saving agents. The literature is replete with such caveats—for example, Greenwood's (1955) concern that social scientists working with social workers be kept on social work's home ground: "Such control is very important, to avoid having social scientists formulate research questions in a manner that impairs their relevance for social work practice" (p. 31).

Despite the literature's recurrent theme of bringing the social back to social work—however one interprets that call—the literature makes abundantly clear that social work has much less fear of the label "junior psychiatrists" than of "junior social scientists." There is some wisdom in this fear, articulated, however, for the wrong reasons. The literature of social work shows considerable confusion about the distinction between a science and a helping art, and the place of social work's "helping theory" and its seemingly immutable principles within that distinction.

Without belaboring the point, it is fair to conclude that social work might find it more valuable to mine the applied potentials of the social sciences than to hold onto its former psychiatric orientation.

It is of some interest that, despite American social welfare programs on behalf of the poor, some 30,000,000 to 40,000,000 or more Americans—the number depending upon one's dollar line of evaluation—live in poverty today. Discussion on behalf of this first client of social work still carries tones of "undeserving," on the one hand, and cries for structural reform, on the other. Social work's ubiquitous tension between the needs of the individual and the demands of the social is also society's tension.

The New Model

The particular model that will best meet social needs must be constructed by social work if it intends to operate as a functional institution. Since there is wide support for the traditional model, despite strains (Hale, 1966, p. 37), there is considerable question about how drastically social work wishes to revise its structure and function.

In *Social Work: The Unloved Profession* (1973), Richan and Mendelsohn see a "new social worker," able to transcend institutional barriers to servicing the client.

Mendelsohn argues that an alliance between the academic and service delivery segments "appears doomed." He would put practice back into the community and eliminate schools of social work in the traditional sense.

Richan sees the solution within the university, with the acquisition of new intellectual underpinnings, with reform coming both from the university and the profession, and intellectual tools from sociology, psychology, and other relevant disciplines.

Time and the public mood, of course, will have a great deal to do with determining social work's final model. In the absence of hindsight, an observer of social work's endless dilemmas will find Richan's general direction more appealing, if that observer is biased toward an eventual alliance between the theoretical and the practical within the university structure.

In point of fact, in the absence of an alternative route to helping as institutionalized as modern social work, it is reasonable to expect that social work will not consider itself obsolete in the immediate future, and that it will continue to be fed by future clientele and student aspirants. In that eventuality, improvement in academic offering is better than no improvement, and the question of what a modest insertion of a sociological framework might do to improve social work's theory is not without relevance.

Put another way, one might speculate about the effects of a minimal alliance with sociology in the early days of American sociology, keeping in mind that the early sociologists of the Chicago School were largely humanitarians interested in legitimizing a new science in an atmosphere that encouraged interrelationships among social workers, sociologists, and members of a variety of other disciplines, including history, political science, philosophy, and psychology (Faris, 1967, pp. 53, 92).

In considering such a contribution, it would be necessary to suppose a reduced emphasis on practice in the two-year Master's program and a greater emphasis on theory, leaving apprenticeship—present-day field work—to the hiring agency.

This solution, then or now, would have the added advantage of freeing social work from the onerous and largely unprofitable task of evaluating psychic aptitudes of student and faculty, while loosening the stranglehold of psychoanalytic compulsion.

Shorter internships throughout the two-year program, such as those now being used in some college programs, would offer educational and vocational experience in the area of the student's choice. Given the nature of the helping art and the great number of new practitioners without the M.S.W., there is no reason to believe that employers cannot make adequate judgments about applicants' suitability for social work jobs requiring certain emotional characteristics, nor that students cannot make their own contribution to such an assessment, nor that employers today are bound by social work assessments.

Nonjudgmentalism

Two long-standing themes of social work theory, and their corresponding limitations in practice, may be used to illustrate the possible corrective contributions of sociology. One of these themes is the principle of *client self-determination;* the other is the closely related principle of *nonjudgmentalism.* Privacy of social work–client relationships is an essential element in both.

What is it to be a nonjudgmental social worker, in view of social work's successive historical choices in favor of helping the deserving poor, the psychically deprived in need of Freudian therapy administered by lay therapists, or, most recently, a variable in a process in need of some vague social structural intervention?

If by *nonjudgmentalism* social work merely means that the social worker does not berate the client for past misfortunes or errors, but accepts the client where he or she is (with a clear and humble eye to social structural conditions) as someone who is to be helped to more satisfying social reality, using the general society's most generous criteria, the use of *nonjudgmentalism* in social work to describe this process is at best confusing, but not harmful. Nonjudgmentalism in this sense is an initial accepting premise, common to professionals generally—doctors, lawyers, teachers—but certainly not explanatory of the science or value system by which the client is to be aided.

In the quasi-technical language of social work this attitude of "neither tolerance nor intolerance" (which, it must be conceded, appears more than a little elusive to the lay mind) is often described as "acceptance." Such acceptance, according to Hollis, is "quite different

137

from approval" of a client's behaviour, and does not "necessitate any giving up of one's own personal code of ethics." (Wootton, 1959, p. 280)

By erecting nonjudgmentalism into a principle above competing principles, social work has denied itself a hardheaded analysis of its own value-function position in terms of the community and, secondarily, has closed itself off from the possibility of exploring newer therapies for client benefit. This principle of nonjudgmentalism also has been social work's main excuse for denying itself involvement in the correctional system—from community prevention through halfway houses—on the grounds that professional nonjudgmentalism makes work in corrections, bound by a legal structure, not casework, and, hence, not compatible with the profession's higher aims (Studt, 1959).

Elliot Studt discusses areas "which have been consistently reported as presenting problems to graduate social workers employed in the correctional field. They are also the correctional tasks which the profession has questioned as part of the social worker's role" (p. 17). These tasks include: investigation and surveillance for the purpose of securing information; the use of controls to modify client behavior; acting as a legal authority person in the client's life with responsibility for value change; and correctional decision making.

On the question of decision making, Studt writes: "It is recognized that all social workers make decisions. There are, however, aspects in decision-making in correctional work which require adaptations by the professional social worker. These seem to lie in the nature of the decisions to be made, the structure of decision-making, and the lack of resources on which the social worker is accustomed to depend in making decisions" (pp. 17–18).

Studt then asks the usual social work questions: What is the nature of the tasks? Why do they present problems of adaptation for graduate social workers? What needs—of system or of client—do these tasks satisfy? Can they be seen as appropriate tasks for the professional social worker and in what way?

The data suggest that social work already has failed the first test of its capacity to deal with the problems of the delinquent, as they have "failed previously to adequately reach the predelinquent, the unmarried mother, the neglectful, rejecting parent, etc. (a failure social workers share with psychiatrists and clinical psychologists)" (Kadushin, 1965, p. 42).

What is surprising is not so much a discovery of failure as the serious attention paid to questions of the appropriateness of problem groups—retardates, dire poverty groups, and delinquents—to social work's task.

In essence, the study by Studt (1959) concludes that social work should get involved in corrections. How effective social work will be hinges on the solution of many problems, stated in a characteristically hesitant and further problem-creating tone: "It is evident in the following analyses that the profession has only begun to break ground in answering these questions. It has been possible to indicate the nature of the difficulties and to establish the relationship of each task to social work responsibility for treatment. Directions in which further study is necessary have also been identified" (p. 18).

The real issues are not so obscure as social work literature portrays them, however complex the problem. The Studt study deals with the question of delinquency as if social work alone, albeit belatedly, had ever considered the problem.

Beginning social work students, before their introduction to the labored literature on nonjudgmentalism, have little trouble discerning that, if social work proclaims to be some type of helping art, the semi-profession, or would-be profession, or technology must have some idea of its change principles. If this is not the case, any claim to special and unique social work knowledge, values, and expertise, including a poorly named "Philosophy of Social Work" course, is a contradiction in terms.

Emphasis on nonjudgmentalism, paradoxically, overlooks the current and historical atmosphere of social work authoritarianism felt by clients, students, and other academics. How can so authoritarian a discipline operate from a principle of nonjudgmentalism?

Client Self-Determination

Considered neither truly social nor inherently truly religious, the client of social work, nonetheless, has been judged to have a right to self-determination.

The literature on client self-determination is voluminous. In 1951, Felix Biestek wrote that, although the principle of client self-determination is one of the most widely held in the field of casework, as far as he could determine, the profession possessed neither a definition nor a comprehensive description of the concept (p. 4). In 1963, Alan Keith-Lucas, in "A Critique of the Principle of Client Self-Determination," concluded that the principle "makes little sense to social work today and could be discarded quite comfortably" (p. 69).

Keith-Lucas questions the " 'professional emphasis on the client's right to self-determination within the limits of reality' as one of the safeguards thrown around a client's 'vulnerability.' "

> Would it not be more realistic to state that the safeguard intended here is the profession's ethical undertaking not to interfere in all those small matters of taste, opinion, and day-to-day living that make one client different from another and give him a sense of being an individual? . . . Why have recourse to a "principle" that has to be modified with words which to a great extent prevent it from being a principle at all? Perhaps if this principle had been given a more realistic name the pro-

fession might have arrived at clearer answers to some important questions, such as by what right and to what extent a social worker should intervene in a client's life. These questions rarely are faced squarely; they are taken care of (as in both Biestek's and Bernstein's articles) by general statements that social workers are "representatives of the community," "allied with social, moral, and legal good," or simply that in some situations the social worker should "try to help" the client change his mind. Any of these statements may be true, but surely they, rather than the ethical bases for man's—any man's, not just a client's —right to decide things for himself, are what needs debating. (pp. 67–68)

Without subscribing to the position that a principle that needs qualification is no principle, one can agree with Keith-Lucas that the particular qualifications that have grown up around the principle of client self-determination, especially the real limitations of client resources, have served in effect to dissipate the principle's usefulness.

How may the principle be stated, and what are its qualifications?

Felix Biestek (1957) says:

One of the firmest convictions of the profession of social work is that the person has an innate ability for self-determination and that a conscious, willful violation of the client's freedom by a caseworker is an unprofessional act which transgresses the client's natural right and impairs casework or makes it impossible. (p. 101)

The principle of client self-determination is the practical recognition of the right and need of clients to freedom in making their own choices and decisions in the casework process. Caseworkers have a corresponding duty to respect that right, recognize that need, stimulate and help to activate that potential for self-direction by helping the client to see and use the available and appropriate resources of the community and of his own personality. The client's right to self-determination, however, is limited by the client's capacity for positive and constructive decision making, by the framework of civil and moral law, and by the function of the agency. (p. 103)

Most important, the client's right of self-determination is limited by the attitudinal and resource climate of the community in which he or she lives. The social work principle of client self-determination is arguable, then, not so much as a beginning principle, but as a preoccupation from which reality considerations largely have been excluded by the profession.

The questions that should have preoccupied social work would have been better stated: How free is the client to be self-determining under the existing legal, agency, and opinion climate in which the nonjudgmental social worker activates the human potential? Indeed, how free has social work's client been to activate personal potential under the profession's helping mystique?

Similarly, to espouse a value of client privacy as primary, without appreciation of corresponding social values and structures, is further to have missed the implications of the reality situation. Neither public relief client nor juvenile delinquent, for example, despite needed safeguards to privacy, has had much chance at a more fundamental privacy of social well-being. The principle of client privacy of communication might have been served better by working to prevent the client from getting involved with the endless recording process of the bureaucratic system, or, once involved, by keeping that process as limited and as painless as possible.

Historically, then, social work's insistence on a unique value system has resulted in what social workers concede is a general vagueness or lack of functionality, with themes such as the search for the generic, the priest-versus-prophet dilemma, nonjudgmentalism, and client self-determination.

In the meantime, social work's historic client has been subjected to means tests, midnight raids, inadequate relief, embarrassing and inept psychological prying, and pseudohealing. Someone once described the process as analogous to a group of dedicated people standing on the bank of a swift-running river, pulling out individual casualties without ever going over to the other bank to see what structural forces were pushing the clients into the water.

Correctional Concepts

At what point of insertion can social work begin to use sociological concepts profitably? George Kelling, M.S.W., in "Caught in a Crossfire of Concepts—Correction and the Dilemmas of Social Work" (1968), suggests one possible opening: "Many of the tensions inherent in social work are most explicit in the field of corrections" (p. 30).

> The dilemmas that confront correctional personnel regarding methodological issues such as the use of authority, value issues such as the concept of self-determination, and the theoretical issues such as the "sickness" versus the "badness" of deviants are not unique to correction, but pervade all areas of social work. Social work has become doctrinaire on the use of authority, social work has oversimplified and overemphasized self-determination, and social work has confused normative and descriptive use of language with its emphasis on the "sickness" of deviants. Correction, because it has dealt with these issues most realistically, can help to reconcile these dilemmas. (p. 26)

In the area of deviance, explored prodigiously by the Chicago School of Sociologists, social work can make use of the sociological frame of reference that sees delinquent children as largely "normal" products of the failure of major socializing institutions of society. (For a corresponding psychiatric view, see Guttmacher, 1958.) It is this viewpoint that placed the problems of delinquents, immigrants, and ghetto residents in a social structural context, turning scholarly attention away from concentration on genetics or personal failure.

This sociological framework was readily available to social workers in the early days of the Chicago School, when cooperation among many disciplines, including social work, was a striking characteristic of the climate at the University of Chicago. That same sociological emphasis, elaborated and refined in a vast literature, still was available and judged functional even after social work had announced its coming of age. See, for example, the massive report by the President's Commission on Law Enforcement and Administration of Justice, *The Challenge of Crime in a Free Society*, especially the section on "Juvenile Delinquency and Youth Crime" (Chapter 3, pp. 55–89), and the Commission's Task Force Report, *Juvenile Delinquency and Youth Crime*, both published in 1967.

The Chicago School approach is unmistakable in the Commission's emphasis on failing institutions in slum areas, the need for a community approach to prevention, and a social view of the delinquent.

> Even if we could identify in advance and deal with those individuals most likely to become delinquent, that would hardly be a sufficient substitute for general shoring up of socializing institutions in the slums. For the fact of the matter is that, whether or not the result in any given case is delinquency, society is failing slum youth. Their families are failing. The schools are failing. The social institutions generally relied on to guide and control people in their individual and mutual existence simply are not operating effectively in the inner city. Instead of turning out men and women who conform to the American norm at least overtly, at least enough to stay out of jail, the slums are producing the highest rates of crime, vice, and financial dependence. By failing these men and woman and, most important, these young people, society wounds itself in many ways. (President's Commission, 1967, p. 59)

Social work's therapeutic view of the delinquent, in this context, has serious shortcomings:

> A long-standing, ubiquitous problem of social workers and psychiatrists of whatever theoretical persuasion has been that of the noninvolvement of their clients or patients. Clients are either disinclined to seek their services or they break off contacts after they have been established, or they respond superficially without showing interest in changing their personal values or life styles. Much of the difficulty stems from the identification of social workers with middle-class values and the invidious moralistic implications of imputing defective personalities to those they try to assist. As a result, barriers to communication often become insurmountable. (President's Commission, Task Force, 1967, pp. 95–96)

As a consequence of social work's inability to see the majority of the delinquents as normally socialized in contra-law subcultures, "comparatively few juvenile court cases are referred to social workers for treatment and many juvenile court judges and probation officers are inhospitable to social workers" (p. 96).

The Task Force Report notes the heavy leaning on Freudian psychiatry by scientific social work, whose tenets the Report credits to Mary Richmond in her early work *Social Diagnosis*. Childhood problems, in this psychobiological and medical orientation, are viewed as symptoms of unresolved Oedipal conflicts. Even with updated versions of socially applied psychoanalysis, treatment is centered on internal emotional life rather than on external acts.

Generally speaking, social workers favor a curtailed dispositional function for the juvenile court. Some doubt that the helping process can be carried on in an authoritarian setting and refuse as clients children adjudicated as wards of the court. Others take the position that treatment should be determined by social work agencies. A smaller number feel that there may be some reconciliation of personal help and authority within the role of the probation officer. Still others, as the Report notes, are not beyond using juvenile court power as a tool for gaining access to clients (p. 95).

Michael Hakeem, in "A Critique of the Psychiatric Approach to the Prevention of Juvenile Delinquency" (1972), points to the powerful influence of psychiatrists, psychologists, social workers, and other psychiatrically oriented personnel in the prevention of juvenile delinquency. He notes the modest influence of sociology in comparison. "As a matter of fact, sociologists, especially those in criminology and corrections have, in the main, subscribed to the psychiatric ideology" (p. 487).

Hakeem quotes Dr. Edward Glover, renowned British psychiatrist and psychoanalyst, writing on behalf of the Institute for the Scientific Treatment of Delinquency. In a memorandum to the Royal Commission on Capital Punishment, Dr. Glover states that the crux of the problem of murder and its prevention lies in an adequate program of testing and guidance, administered at the proper age. Although, theoretically, this may be at any age, says Dr. Glover, in practice, the optimal age is between 2½ and 8 years. Dr. Glover proposes that such a program, while not sufficient to recognize all potential murderers—"a foolish claim"—would strike seriously at the root of the problem (p. 489).

The problems of children, however complex, still are a relatively uncluttered reflection of the problems social work must face with its client group. It is in this area that social work might be urged to start inserting material from the social sciences, especially sociology. It is noteworthy that social work has had special problems with the concept of deviance throughout its history—in its client groups, students, faculty, private practitioners, paraprofessionals, other disciplines, and critics who refuse to accept social work's claim to a special type of knowledge and expertise in the face of countless failures and an admitted lack of a theoretical foundation. It is precisely in a cultural context that deviancy must be seen and understood.

In re Gault, 1967

No one seriously associated with the juvenile correctional process would propose that any discipline, including sociology, has the problem and solution in true focus. This point, however, is not at issue. What is at issue is social work's seeming inability to see the child involved (Luther Burbank's most sensitive of all organisms, 1907) as worthy of serious professional attention rather than professional posturing.

When professions do not agree on the solution to a problem, it still is possible to pick pathways that offer more realistic hope of solution. While social work was worrying about its particular place in the correctional process, the difficulty of borrowing, and the problems of graduate students in handling the demands of the correctional framework, other assessments continued to be made.

The Task Force Report on *Juvenile Delinquency and Youth Crime* notes: "The ideal of therapeutic treatment found its way into juvenile court philosophy from social work and psychiatry, its pervasiveness measurable by the extent to which persons educated and trained in social work have indirectly influenced the juvenile court or moved into probation and correctional officer positions" (p. 95). By 1965, however, the therapeutic model was being questioned very seriously by those familiar with the results of research on effectiveness undertaken by disciplines other than social work. The particular marriage of the judicial and administrative which became the first juvenile court in the world in Chicago in 1899 was showing signs of unanticipated consequences, following the initial worldwide acclaim of its potential.

At least as early as 1949, when social work was settling into its new-found Freudianism, Paul W. Tappan, sociologist and attorney, presented an analysis and criticism of the deprivation of children's rights by the juvenile courts—a criticism that was to be, in essence, the conclusion of the Supreme Court of the United States in two decisions many years later, *Kent* (1966) and *Gault* (1967).

In March 1966, in the case of Morris A. Kent, Jr., the Supreme Court issued its famous "Crack of Kent" warning. Justice Abe Fortas, in the majority opinion, expressed concern that children before juvenile courts may receive "neither the protections accorded to adults nor the solicitous care and regenerative treatment postulated for children." This decision applied only to the District of Columbia, but it was the first time the Court had criticized juvenile court procedures.

In May 1967, in its decision *In re Gault*, the Supreme Court granted juveniles a number of rights accorded to adult offenders: suitable notice of pending charges, the right to counsel, protection of the privilege against self-incrimination in court and during official interrogation, and the right of confrontation and cross-examination. By this decision, the Court literally revolutionized one aspect of the handling of deviancy, with no major input from institutionalized social work. The court, in effect, firmly placed the juvenile in a social context of civil rights, rejecting the notion that well-intended, but often ineffective or harmful, therapeutic intervention justified the deprivation of the legal rights of the child.

The implications of *Gault* have not yet been realized throughout the United States. It takes no gift of prescience, however, to realize that social work's long love affair with the case history, an essential element of its oldest method, will need some modification to meet new standards of evidence in the adjudication of delinquency by the juvenile court. The modification will be necessarily in the direction of better data gathering and less unwarranted psychiatric evaluation, regardless of benign intentions on behalf of the child's total good. The vision of social detective which Mary Richmond sometimes inspired, as well as the aim of psychic physician that later social workers held as valid, will need to be improved by some model of scientific inquiry that meets legal requirements.

Gault also has implications, though not intended as such, for the social work tradition of establishing a relationship with the client. For children, the social work "relationship" can and often does become "The Lie of Professional Helpfulness" (Halleck, 1966). This is especially true in the correctional area, if the child is urged to tell all on the mistaken assumption that the social worker is able to sweep away the limitations of the reality situation by means of the relationship. Adult clients, except for the most unwary, undoubtedly have learned this truth, even if social workers have not.

Relational therapy, however, is not the only alternative. When the needs of the community conflict with those of the adolescent, notes Halleck, it is the community that must be obeyed. Within that limitation, it is still possible for the social worker to identify himself as someone who wants to help the adolescent. He is being dishonest, however, if he does not communicate, at the same time, that one of his basic roles is other than help-oriented (p. 283).

Watertight Compartments

In the year the Supreme Court handed down the *Gault* decision, the *Social Service Review* continued the long discussion on the education of the social worker in an article on "The Teacher in Education for Social Work." Inevitably, the author (Younghusband, 1967) finds insuperable problems in borrowing from other disciplines.

"How?" and "What?" are of equal importance. Our failure to analyze what good practice means has been matched by lack of sufficient interest in how adult students learn, compared with concentration on what we think they should be taught. What they are taught is sometimes an uneasy compromise between social work teachers and some lecturers in other subjects who are more interested in teaching a basic course than in discovering what social work students need and how to relate different subjects effectively to each other. For instance, a course in law may be almost purely factual and a concurrent course in sociology contain nothing about law as a form of social control and an expression of social attitudes. The result is that sometimes so-called integrating seminars have to help students to see the interrelationships between one subject and another when initial joint planning in the light of objectives could have prevented these watertight compartments from the beginning. (pp. 361–362)

In the world of reality, the process of social thought does not occur with perfect integration. The mesh of social science framework and legal principles reflected in the *Gault* case is a good illustration. As a result, social work's plea for integrated placebos for students on the Master's level unfortunately sounds too much like past social work complaints that the job of borrowing is too complex to be left in the hands of the lenders. There is no evidence to suggest that predigestion of scientific principles by social workers, to be endlessly regurgitated in the classroom by social workers, will best serve the students' task of integration. It is safer to assume that students at that level will do their own integration, if only by rejection.

The Sociological Framework

If sociology does not possess a complete theory of social change, as social workers have noted rightly, it does have a framework for the study of social problems, based on studies of social class and built around the concepts of differential social organization and differential social risk (Merton and Nisbet, 1971, v–ix). It is on the effect of social structure on the individual that social work and sociology parted company shortly after their respective beginnings, both in England and in the United States.

Of all the areas of social work functioning, it is clearest in the area of juvenile corrections that social work's previous choices in the direction of psychiatry and an exaggerated professionalism "have subtly pushed social work into another ball game in another park . . . divorced from the culture in which we live, which is doing more to people than are their psychic maladjustments" (D. Hunter, 1964, p. 595).

Social work's ball game in the field of corrections looks amateurish and posturing because it ignores the concepts of social class and differential social opportunity—concepts that sociologists have developed extremely well. Hunter suggests that social work has not understood the concept of social class very well in the first place, and this "blind spot" has frustrated much sincere effort. "The primary victims of this have been case workers who have labored to establish communication, to nurture insight, and to stimulate movement in a lower class family with little success" (p. 599).

Too limited in its field of choice, social work "has shopped too exclusively at the stores of the psychic sciences and too rarely dropped in at the supermarket to select from the sociology, political science, anthropology, social psychology, and economic shelves" (p. 598).

A starting point for inserting social science content into the social work curriculum might be, very simply, the exploration, historical and empirical, of the concepts of social class, differential social organization, and differential social risk.

> Social work training and agency practice must pay more attention to class and culture: what they are; what they mean in terms of values; how people in different class and culture spheres look at things differently; what this means in terms of differential response to social work techniques which have been developed perhaps too "culture free." We wish IQ tests could be more culture free; not so social work techniques. (Hunter, 1964, pp. 599–600)

Stated differently, social workers should approach juvenile problems in terms of what R. G. Barker has called the world of the "absent organism": they should ask what certain environments can be expected to produce, given the social values of the society, irrespective of the organism's response (Barker, 1961; see also Bossard and Boll, 1960).

Without denying the rich potential for collaboration among the sciences and arts dealing with human problems, the reason that social work should look to sociology today is not, as Kadushin (1959) has suggested, because sociology has moved closer to psychiatry and psychiatry has moved closer to the social sciences. Rather, it is precisely in those areas where sociology sees the effect of the social structure on the individual in sharply different terms from psychiatry (Merton, 1938) that sociology can serve as a corrective. Although the sociological and psychological viewpoints are moving closer in analysis of criminological data, these two schools of thought nevertheless represent two distinct and contradictory views of causation and rehabilitation at their polar points (Sutherland, 1955, p. 58).

Social work already has had too much psychiatric orientation. It badly needs the balance of a social structural perspective, with social structure seen as independent variable. Social work should be alerted to the possibilities of nonpsychiatric services for the greater bulk of its clientele—in criminology, for those 75–80% of deviants who form a dysocial group, the "normal" criminal who has responded to defective cultural process in an essentially normal way (Guttmacher, 1958).

With some justification, social workers on occasion have explained their professional dilemmas simply as adaptations of a profession to the changing demands and miserly limitations imposed by the culture in which social work functions. Other disciplines have responded similarly—notably, sociology, in its early bias in social problem analysis toward the rural, homogenous community as good and organized and the emerging city as somehow bad and disorganized (Mills, 1943). The bias was corrected, however, and the city became a laboratory of study for the sociologists and students of the Chicago School.

The fact is that there is material to be borrowed from the social sciences, and specifically from sociology, which would have the effect of bringing social work closer to the present reality situation. Whatever the difficulties, social work protests too much.

The Scientific Spirit

Gilbert Geis, a sociologist, suggests an even more fundamental reason why social work should look to the social sciences.

> A guild rule of sociology is the principle that practitioners approach a problem as an "if-then" sequence; that is, if one takes certain steps, certain consequences will ensue; or, vice versa, if one wishes to produce certain results, one may, on the basis of past experience or present research, be able to indicate the methods and techniques to bring them about. (1965, p. 28)

In this process, "fact must be distinguished from fancy, folklore from truth, and preference from inference" (p. 28).

In a very early work on *The Scientific Spirit and Social Work* (1919), Arthur James Todd, Ph.D., Professor of Sociology and Director of the Training Course for Social and Civic Work at the University of Minnesota, asked questions and suggested conclusions with a strongly contemporary ring of common sense.

What is social work, Todd asked, that movement "born of a sense of responsibility to society," as the report of the Committee on Education for Social Work at a National Conference of Charities described it?

> But that statement does not bring us very far on the road to knowing what social work really is. Is it charity? Is it social reform? Is it doing for other people what they cannot do for themselves? If you applied for membership in a Social Workers' Club and gave any or all of these qualifications, would you be accepted? Nobody knows. At any rate, the definitions they imply are vague enough. If you turn, say to that great decennial encyclopedia, the United States Census, you will

be plunged into even deeper darkness, for in it you will find social workers pigeonholed with such semiprofessional pursuits as abstractors, notaries, justices of the peace, fortune tellers, hypnotists, spiritualists, etc. (sic!), healers (except physicians and surgeons), officials of lodges, societies, etc., religious workers, keepers of penal institutions, theatrical owners, managers, and officials. (Todd, 1919, p. 63)

"We may assume, then, with considerable assurance that social work not only is, but sets for itself a huge and intricate problem. Whether it is a fully fledged profession or only a profession in the making is of no importance to the present discussion. The real point is that the scientific spirit is necessary to social work whether it is a real profession or only a go-between craft. The cat is now out of the bag, but where has she jumped" (p. 66)?

If Todd, in 1919, saw the necessity for incorporating the scientific spirit, the present-day observer can only echo agreement. The cat is indeed out of the bag. As to where she has jumped, she could do worse than to follow Todd's early reasoning regarding the nature and direction of social work.

But I still believe there is such a thing. It must, however, be stated in broader terms. And it can be. A bulletin of the New York School of Philanthropy defines social work as "any form of persistent and deliberate effort to improve living or working conditions in the community, or to relieve, diminish, or prevent distress, whether due to weakness of character or to pressure of external circumstances." We might go a step further . . . and say that social work ought to stand for organizing scientifically the forces, personal and material of a community in such a way as to eliminate waste and friction, and to raise progressively the capacity of every member for productivity, service, and joy in life. (pp. 64-65)

"But, you may say, that is simply applied or practical sociology. That, to my way of thinking is precisely what it is; and that is why 'social work' and the 'scientific spirit' must always be linked in theory and practice" (p. 65).

Todd's description of social work's function in fact repeats the call for training not in science, but in the scientific attitude—a call originally issued in the Introductory Lecture on Curriculum of the School of Sociology of the Charitable Organisation Society.

If social work claims it has lost an early wisdom, the same "wisdom" keeps cropping up throughout social work's history from diverse sources. The lament for a lost wisdom would be better phrased as the loss of a sensible starting principle. Todd's quaint phrases, for example, are in many ways more illuminating than later social work formulations that place social work "somewhere in the helping environment" and define social work's client as a variable in a process.

Viewing social work from Todd's 1919 perspective confirms the impression that much of the complexity that social work envisages in each helping task is of social work's own making.

Todd's position has several distinct advantages. He sees part of social work's task as educational, a position which social work underplays. He recognizes the need for generalized social work knowledge without sacrificing division of labor, a point social work missed in its vain search for the all-embracing generic. He draws clear distinctions between science and art, and lightly dismisses the preoccupation with the exact professional status of social work.

For Todd, social work has three aims—he calls them the "three chief crops": the spread of socialized intelligence; alleviative and remedial work on behalf of the subnormal or handicapped members of the community; organized prevention against adverse and depressive forces in the community (p. 65).

Science, he concludes, does not claim to have complete knowledge of the truth nor to have established perfect order out of chaos in this world. "It is less an accomplished fact than an attitude. . . . Hence, in connecting science with social work, our aim is not so much immediate results as an attitude of mind; for, as Huxley pointed out, 'The scientific spirit is of more value than its products, and irrationally held truths may be more harmful than reasoned errors' " (pp. 71–72).

Social work's present historical choice, perhaps its last, is the acquisition of this scientific spirit. Todd expresses the potential benefits as well as anyone: "The scientific spirit does away with obtrusive personality; it pours a healthy astringent upon one's ego. It broadens our sense of personality until we get the idea firmly fixed that we are merely representing the best thought of the community and are not exploiting our own vanity upon the poor and the needy. This is a very subtle temptation and can only be met by rigorous scientific self-immolation" (p. 81).

More Than Sociology

A case having been made for the benefits of sociology in the formulation of social work theory, it is clear that a good case also can be made for including the social sciences generally—cultural anthropology, political science, economics—as well as for including courses in law, and for undergraduate education of social workers in the broad liberal arts tradition.

Seeing the cultural animal in the common wisdom of humanity would help to break the narrowly conceived framework of pathology within which the social worker has become accustomed to viewing the world. Such a conception of social work education, however, would preclude the present attitude toward the student's academic past: "The first problem encountered by the social work educator, as well as by the student, is the nature of the break with the student's academic past. Dr. Charles Frankel has identified this break as a major problem of all professional schools. . . . One question is the extent to which this turn to action represents a complete break or carries with it some elements of the earlier academic orientation. The apparent opinion of the social work schools is partly expressed by the rapidity with which the student is moved into the field compared with the amount of classroom time" (E. Walsh, 1965, p. 50).

Because of social work's too willing quest for professional identity along the lines of medicine and psychiatry, the rich resource of students' experience of life in groups, their own and others, has remained untapped. Their previous experience requires augmentation and refinement, not the total resocialization found in mental hospitals or correctional institutions. It should be noted that, as of 1963, 44% of incoming students were married or previously married, 23% were practicing parents, and 83% had had some prior experience in social work or a clearly related activity, most of this experience in full-time paid employment in social work (Kadushin, 1965, p. 39).

What is not being suggested is the type of approach represented by "The Humanities and Social Work Education," a paper presented at the Council for Social Work Education Fourteenth Annual Program Meeting in New York in 1966 (Greene, 1966). Essentially a casework didactic of social work insights in selections of literature, this approach calls for new bravery (as social workers are fond of terming their adventures into unknown territory), this time not from the social scientist observer, but from the teacher of the humanities.

And, whether he is to be a teacher or social worker, he needs the tempering that accompanies confrontation during what Erikson calls the "psycho-social moratorium." He needs to dredge up the queer, unanswerable questions which are philosophical, so that he can orient himself in the days to come, find his own perspective, and become as clear as he knows how to be—and as cool.

This is what it means to be enlisted in the search for meaning at a moment when meanings are no longer fixed. This is what it means to be enlisted in the quest for principle and ideal, when the codes are no longer "given." Perhaps, by consulting disciplines ordinarily strange to schools of social work, teachers can provide significant occasions for enlistment. And some day, making his existential choice on the street, in an agency, on a tenement stoop, a student may discover that his teacher (who will never know) has set him free to be. (p. 31)

By all means set the student free, but let this process remain, traditionally, with the humanities teacher, to set the student free to be—a social worker, if he or she so chooses. Moreover, the psychosocial moratorium should be reserved for adolescents, as Erikson intended, not transposed onto graduate students or teachers. At a conference sponsored by the Children's Bureau of the Department of Health, Education, and Welfare, Erikson (1955) pointed out that our society offers the young person two choices in place of a psychosocial moratorium: delinquency status or the status of needing psychiatric help. The conference—at which Erikson represented the psychological science and Merton, the sociological—was convened precisely because the Bureau was convinced that we know more theoretically than we put into practice on the behalf of the juvenile delinquent.

As director of a Master of Social Work group research project, the author was both amused and dismayed to find second-year graduate students fully expecting to find detailed analyses of vague psychosocial patternings in case histories submitted by school social workers, each of whom had some 3,000 students as clients in preventive and rehabilitative efforts in the city's most severe poverty area. Let us have a moratorium on the teaching of naive professional expectations.

According to Titmuss (1958), "only now are we beginning to grope our way towards some scientific understanding of society. . . . Uncertainty, then, is part of the price that has to be paid for being interested in the many-sidedness of human needs of behaviour" (p. 14). If this is so, social work cannot afford to be less certain than common sense, on the one hand, or the best scientific evidence, on the other. Where uncertainty exists, doubt should not be erected into a rigidly dogmatic practical art.

To imagine, for example, that the mayor of a large city will sit idly by while social work considers him a potential client in a community organization project, as one educator fondly hoped, is, as Hunter observed, to be in another ball game.

The modern ball game calls for different rules. "Modern man," Karl Mannheim (1946) concludes, "prefers to have his rights and duties clearly defined, rather than to receive a personal favor"; he prefers that his "personal affairs should be treated impersonally." In his most thoughtful and humane discussions, modern man favors institutional solutions that move toward "classless justice" (p. 322).

If social work's previous options have pushed it into another ball game, in another ball park, often divorced from the surrounding culture, it is because previous choices have shut out the profession from an understanding of differential social risk, a concept whose ramifications would have suggested a less personal and more even-handed service.

Society will demand more from the profession's future broadening excursions into the humanities than the following conclusion, reached in 1966, when social work already had announced its coming of age:

> Only recently have most of us confronted the impossibility of anyone no matter how healthy, clever, or "well-adjusted," leading a really

152

good life in the midst of poverty. Only now, both in teacher training and social work education, are we coming to terms with our own limitations. Neither teachers nor social workers can do what is really necessary: effect the kinds of changes that will do away with disadvantage, underprivilege, and the multiple pathologies that spring from the root cause, poverty, which we cannot, in our professional roles, do much about. (Greene, 1966, p. 30)

End and Beginning

The journey through social work's past has brought us back to 1969, the centennial year, with special emphasis on the years since 1965, when the profession proclaimed its maturity as a helping art. New directions since that time presumably will be reflected in a new literature. Future assessment may use the same method employed in looking backward to beginnings—namely, taking social workers at their word when they describe successes, failures, dilemmas, and syntheses of major themes.

This tracing of broad themes has not permitted discussion of the individual efforts of the many social workers who have escaped the mystique of their profession, nor the innovative thrust of the many students of social work who appear wiser than their teachers.

The effectiveness of social work in the future will depend on those who refuse to be deflected from the reality situation by the award of "professionalism." If too few are willing to accept this challenge, the Chemung County Evaluation of Casework Service will continue to be repeated:

In this rigorously designed, objective pretest-posttest attempt to measure the effectiveness of trained social casework service per se to dependent multiproblem families within the framework of a public assistance agency, no statistically significant difference could be found between the demonstration and control groups. Or, taking research as well as casework factors into consideration, an ultra-objective statement might be that whatever was done by these trained caseworkers, under these conditions and in this setting, cannot be demonstrated, on the basis of the particular measures we chose to apply, to have had an appreciable effect. (Wallace, 1967, p. 389)

FORWARD TO 1990

Over a decade has passed since modern social work passed the 100th anniversary of its founding, with a remarkable reticence about its roots. In America an enthusiastic "coming of age" in 1965 became a serious crisis in the 70's. In 1979 when most of 3,000 British social workers concluded their six-month strike, the public made its own assessment, as devastating a critique as any content analysis of social workers' own statements. Criticism ranged from "inadequate" to "harmful" ministrations.

The *Sunday Telegraph* (September 16, 1979), reporting on a research project done for the Department of Health and Social Welfare on social worker activities, concluded that social workers spend more than half their working hours at conferences, meetings, and desk jobs. Less than 30% of their time was spent with clients.

The strike halted social work departments in 14 areas, many of London's poorest boroughs. The strike, however, did not produce calamities strikers claimed. Tower Hamlets has decided not to replace 60 of the striking workers.

In a later two-year study Dr. Colin Brewer, psychiatrist, concluded a Royal Commission inquiry is essential, because it is arguable whether social work as constituted is particularly helpful. Most of the studies showed that specific training does not make for more effective social work, training serving the interests more of the trainers than trainees.

Chairman of the British Association of Social Workers Elwyn Owens warned that the profession was dogged by a "pervasive sense of anger and helplessness." His report claimed social workers have been given inadequate training and resources. Further, inquiries into child abuse tragedies "showed repeatedly" that there is a gap between what social workers do and what the public think they do.

And what of America? What new insights emerged in the official literature of the 70's?

It is well to repeat that since I was dealing with official concerns, I have not discussed sociological works which undoubtedly found their way into classrooms: *Delinquency and Opportunity: A Theory of*

Delinquent Gangs (1960) by Richard A. Cloward and Lloyd E. Ohlin of the New York School of Social Work of Columbia University and *Delinquent Boys: The Culture of the Gang* (1955) by Albert K. Cohen. I felt description of the earlier Chicago School made for better illustration. Further, I share Herbert A. Bloch's assessment (Preface, Martin and Fitzpatrick, 1964) that Cohen's theory provides limited leverage and that "recent interest in Cloward and Ohlin's theory of 'structural opportunities' (based largely upon the theoretical formulations of Robert K. Merton and the classical work of Emile Durkheim) provides little active support for the skills of social control, despite efforts to superimpose such theories upon extensive community programs" (p. vi).

By 1973, as noted previously, social work change was such that Richan and Mendelsohn felt constrained to publish *Social Work: The Unloved Profession.* Mendelsohn stated that an alliance between academic and service delivery segments "appears doomed," and opted for putting practice into the community and eliminating traditional schools of social work as we know them. Richan focused on the need for new intellectual underpinnings, with reform from the university and profession and the use of intellectual tools from sociology, psychology, and related disciplines.

1977: 108 Years of History

The lead article in the *Journal of Education for Social Work* for Spring 1977 proposes "a beginning 'map' for analyzing components in learning and teaching in social work education" (Bloksberg and Lowy, 1977, p. 3). The authors' comments are a further examination of *Integrative Learning and Teaching in Schools of Social Work,* a demonstration project involving eight schools of social work (Lowy, Bloksberg, and Walberg, 1971).

This beginning "map" is concerned primarily with analyzing the environment in which social work education takes place, a previously neglected area. A major educational objective continues to be that students should learn—"in the fullest sense of the word—those concepts, skills, and values deemed appropriate by the educational system" (Bloksberg and Lowy, 1977, p. 3).

The authors deem it necessary to emphasize such commonsensical assumptions as "it is desirable that learning be integrated" (p. 3) and "that integrated learning requires integrated teaching" (p. 4). "Though social work is characterized more by an absence of cognitive structure," they point to Bruner's dictum directing social work "to impose a theoretical framework upon that which is taught" (p. 5).

There is nothing in the Winter and Spring 1977 issues of the *Journal*, nor, indeed, in any previous issues of the 1970s, to suggest that the state of theoretical and practical synthesis so ardently desired by the profession has been achieved. This remains the case despite the adoption, in November 1969, by the Board of Directors of the Council on Social Work Education of a new Curriculum Policy Statement, effective January 1, 1971, for Master's degrees in Social Work, to be used as a basis for evaluating new schools being considered for accreditation or older ones for reaffirmation of accredited status.

In 1977, Hockenstad observes: "Social work educators face a major challenge in defining their role in training for the human services" (p. 57). He recalls the 1966 challenge issued to social work by John Gardner, then Secretary of Health, Education, and Welfare, who envisioned the profession in 1990 as offering a hospitable academic home to theoreticians and students of social policy.

> It is now over 10 years later with fewer than 13 to go until 1990. The peaks identified in the 1960's remain unclimbed, although base camps have been established. Now is the time for social work education to move up the mountain of interdisciplinary training in the human services. The challenge is evident and our immediate response is critical. (Hockenstad, 1977, p. 59)

Return to Social Problems

If, in the spring of 1965, the *Journal* announced social work's "coming of age" as a profession, in the spring of 1970 it was the harbinger of hopeful signs of a new movement: "The articles in this issue make abundantly clear that schools of social work in the United States are increasingly moving on a path of radically altering the locus of concern and mode of the profession. The emphasis upon a macro-orientation toward social problems is now reflected in the curricula of many schools" (p. 2).

Not everyone was so optimistic. Joseph L. Vigilante, D.S.W., reviewing *Changing Services for Changing Clients*, published for the National Association of Social Workers by Columbia University Press in 1969, warns: "If anyone seriously holds the belief that much of social work is rapidly moving away from direct treatment into the realm of planning administration, research, and the management of human services, let him not be deluded, for the book of writings of five professional experts offers very little supportive evidence that this is the trend" (Spring 1970, p. 81).

Similarly, in the fall of 1970, the *Journal* noted Kurt Reichart's "rather authoritatively" stated observation that the era of ordering social work practice in terms of the familiar triad of casework, group work, and community organization was coming to an end, as a sign of changes that "provoke anxiety as well as hope" (p. 2).

In summary, the early 1970s found social work formally returning full circle to an interest in social problems, the focus of the earliest schools of social work, but returning at a still "early stage" of its "common base." Harriett M. Bartlett, in the 1971 edition of the *Encyclopedia of Social Work*, observed: "The idea of the common base is still at an early stage and requires further development. Particularly needed is a clearer idea regarding social work's focus, its area of central concern, which must occupy a key position in any frame of reference for the profession" (p. 1479).

By 1977, there still was no significant consensus on the question of focus, or core. Since the original problem offerings of the first schools, the search had been complicated by heightened professional self-consciousness and a proliferation of course offerings and degree programs, in social work and in new practice areas. Further, the knowledge base from which social work must draw literally has exploded. Duehn and Mayadas (1977) concluded: "Social work education is confronted with a divergence of opinion on the nature of graduate training programs, with specific reference to the identification of practice-related competency criteria at entrance and exit points of the educational process" (p. 22).

Some Positives and Negatives

Despite admission of failure by social workers in finding a common core of subject matter and unique identity, the current literature does reveal some positive signs, along with evidence of persistent shortcomings.

The literature still contains repetition of such favorite angst-provoking themes as the search for the generic; a continuing preoccupation with the professional identity of social workers; a sing-song of "values, attitudes, and skills"; and ambivalence, both overt and covert, about the place of the burgeoning group of "social work types" lacking formal degrees, especially as they threaten social work's self-confidence.

The literature of 1977 also still reveals areas in which social workers seem to have been recruited from a tree far distant from the garden of general human concern and common sense knowledge. In an article emphasizing "The Necessity of Linguistic Sophistication for Social Workers" (1977), which means the need to inject English language study into the social work curriculum for the benefit of middle-class social workers who deal with lower-class clients, Elin

J. and John D. Cormican observe: "Similarly, how much more effective would it be if social work supervisors and instructors have sophistication in language. . . . Rather than judging a person as ignorant because of leaving the *d* off past tense forms, as in 'the client was suppose to come,' would it not be more positive for the supervisor to understand this as a dialectical quirk rather than stupidity" (p. 21)?

"Fieldwork Preparation for Entrance into Mental Retardation Practice" (Cramer, 1977) represents the same social work professional obtuseness. The *Journal* editors preface this article by noting that a beginning has been made in regarding the mentally retarded as "people of worth and dignity in our society," and suggesting that social work is endeavoring to find ways to bring significant service to this group. The article goes on to indulge in a type of self-congratulation hardly worthy of a profession:

> One substantive evidence of change is being demonstrated by graduate and undergraduate social work students who accept field placement in agencies serving the mentally retarded. In addition to the implied stigma of working in an institutionalized setting, there is a particular stigma attached to working in the institutions for the mentally retarded. Not only have many social workers been reluctant to enter this specialization, but administrators and others in authoritative policy-making positions tend not to include qualified social workers on the staff of such institutions. Fortunately the practice is changing in some parts of the country. (pp. 37–38)

Nevertheless, the literature does look livelier. Blacks, Chicanos, and American Indians show up in discussion—even if one article on helping the disadvantaged focuses on training North American Indians as social workers, certainly not their root problem. The methodological vocabulary of social systems is in evidence, although the analyses tend to be on a level of abstraction that would give little comfort to the practicing social worker, who presumably already knows that there are institutions, interconnections, and larger social systems.

I found two very good discussions of the rights of the social work student: Frank Peirce's "Student Involvement: Participatory Democracy or Adult Socialization?" (1970) and Joseph Vigilante's "Student Participation in Decision-Making in Schools of Social Work" (Fall 1970).

Peirce addresses the problem of role confusion, most apparent in the status of students—and, by implication, of faculty. He concludes that, of four purposes noted in the "Joint Statement on the Rights and Freedoms of Students" of the American Association of University Professors (1967), "it seems that the moral and emotional education development of students, or student socialization, has been valued most and received the major emphasis.

"In large measure, this emphasis has resulted from the failure of social work educators in the classroom and in the field to recognize and value the student as anything more than a 'young life' or potential recruit to be molded into some preferred image for 'responsible entry into practice' " (p. 21).

The word on students probably will continue to go forth, even without explicit recognition of Elliott Dunlap Smith's caution in the mid-1950s:

> The problem of bringing powerful and creative minds to social work is complicated by the fact that social work places an exceptional premium on balanced personalities and on negative qualities such as absence of irritability, or self-assertiveness, or even of the creative maladjustment which has played such a major part in the progress of mankind. (1957, p. 4)

Armand Lauffer (1971), in a study of 2,766 students, describes the new breed of community organization student as more intelligent, better prepared academically, and more independent. That the majority of the new breed in this study are men, as compared with the female domination of the older casework and group work, also may be a hopeful sign, if we can expect them to be balanced by more assertive female social workers in the future.

As another force for change, Douglas Glasgow (1971) has described "The Black Thrust for Vitality: The Impact on Social Work Education" as "the most serious crisis within the network of social work institutions" (p. 9).

Thus, there is room for optimism regarding a different student socialization and impact on the curriculum, despite the results of a study reported by Arthur Cryns in 1977. Based on a sample of 136 social work students at a large Eastern state university, Cryns found that social work practice experience was not related in any consistent manner to the attitudinal traits measured (p. 47).

"This would suggest that the education they receive does not elevate their cultural capacities so that they become less susceptible to stereotyped, and perhaps prejudiced, notions about those they will assist" (p. 49). In this study, undergraduate students manifested a consistently more positive appreciation of human motives than did graduate students, a phenomenon analogous to data found in medical schools and clinical psychology training programs.

1960s Seen As Crisis

What does emerge in the literature of the 1970s is an acknowledgment of the crisis of the 1960s. It was this atmosphere of the 1960s that prompted my own journey backward into social work literature.

Though current analyses of this crisis still show evasiveness, particularly with regard to the inability to come to grips with social science directions, nevertheless the situation has been acknowledged and discussed in the literature as a crisis.

In 1973, the International Association of Schools of Social Work published the *World Guide to Social Work Education*, a comparative analysis of 79 schools of social work in 65 countries. The *Guide* was a second attempt by the profession at an international comparative review, following the United Nations publication of *Training for Social Work: An International Survey* in 1950, according to Katherine A. Kendall, secretary-general of the International Association, who commented on the *Guide* at the Seventeenth International Congress of Schools of Social Work, held in Nairobi, Kenya, in 1974:

> The *World Guide* appeared at the right moment. The 1950s were a placid although highly productive period for social work education. Schools of social work were established for the first time throughout the developing world. Old schools consolidated their programs and worked hard at realizing the goals of educating, not just for jobs or specialties, but for the total profession. There was growing dissatisfaction in many parts of the world, expressed by faculty but more openly by students, with the nature, content, and outcome of social work education. The need for change was almost everywhere proclaimed. (1974/1977, p. 76)

By 1972, says Kendall, "the results of critical analysis and reorientation of educational programs had begun to emerge," even though program content still contained "much of the curriculum content of the 1950s and 1960s" (pp. 76–77).

Present course listings of schools of social work do show an amazing proliferation since the 1960s. Kendall, however, questions the significance of these new offerings: "Much has been said in the last decade about flexibility, diversity, and variety in social work education. . . . Do the facts as represented in the course listings support these proclamations of change" (p. 80)?

Except for a few countries, primarily in Latin America, "the answer is 'no, not as clearly as one would expect.' However, upon further reflection and more detailed study of curriculum materials, it is possible to risk an explanation that embraces both continuity and a number of new directions."

> Social work education has indeed, changed, but this has taken place within a curriculum framework that has varied little over the years. . . .
>
> What, then, is new in the social work education of the 1970s? Course titles, which frequently hide more than they reveal, do not give us the answer. There are clues in the information on field instruction, and, as already noted, the educational objectives of many schools express more clearly than their curricular offerings the nature of the change that is taking place. (p. 80)

Then There Is Social Science

The most significant change in course offerings, according to Kendall (1974/1977), lies in the area of social development.

> A major change lies in the kinds of background knowledge that we now draw from the social and behavioral sciences. It is a far cry from the "notions of sociology" of an earlier era to "general systems theory"; from "notions of economics" to the "economics of development." We are keenly aware of an explosion of knowledge in the social sciences which naturally gives us more content from which to select. (pp. 80–81)

What weight is this new knowledge given as a component in the curriculum? "It is significant today that content is selected not primarily for the general enlightenment of students on the nature of man and society but for the express purpose of guiding professional activity.... Social science content is sought not as an end in itself but as a means to deepen understanding of specific problem situations" (p. 81).

This use of the social sciences surely accounts for the paucity of articles dealing with substantive synthesis in the social sciences in the *Journal of Education for Social Work* in the 1970s. Here, the method is indeed the message, with article after article bearing the dead millstone weight of "Implications for Social Work," ranging from "Spirit and Substance: Beginnings in the Education of Radical Social Workers" (Hunter and Soleeby, 1977) to a discussion of the philosophy of science. (Incidentally, the reference to "radical" social workers is in no way linked to neo-Marxist philosophy, pro or con. The critical issue here for the graduate school is to "somehow put the student in closer touch with himself" [p. 61].)

Actually, the new Curriculum Policy Statement made effective in 1971 merely comes to the conclusion that there is no generally accepted unified theory of human behavior (Horowitz, 1971, p. 43). Further, administration and research are no longer included as distinct entities, but rather woven into the curriculum in general, with Horowitz, for one, having "some reservations as to whether research can be taught in this manner" (p. 43). Under the new policy, it is conceivable that "one single course could include knowledge covering Social Welfare Policy and Services, Human Behavior and Social Environment and Practice if some scheme for structuring was developed" (Katz, 1971, p. 49).

Willard C. Richan has come to terms with the profession by participating in the establishment of a new school of social work "conceived in relative liberty and dedicated to the proposition that all traditions are up for grabs. The times are especially auspicious for such a venture, for the Council on Social Work Education is saying 'right on!' in its new Curriculum Policy Statement" (1971, p. 55). About that Policy Statement, Richan writes that, up to 1971,

162

schools of social work have decided, for all practical purposes, who is to be a professional social worker. "Therefore, the curriculum policies of the Council on Social Work Education have a deserved role in defining 'professionalism' in our field. I submit that the new Curriculum Policy Statement, while it offers exciting possibilities—indeed, may be the only viable policy for these uncertain times—does not provide such a definition" (p. 57).

Though Kendall (1974/1977) sees the possibility of laying a groundwork in policy, planning, and administration with supporting knowledge from the social and behavioral sciences for all students in the basic program, she asks that social workers not delude themselves that all schools could or should produce full-blown policy makers and planners from the basic program (pp. 81–82).

Kendall goes on to elaborate other problems, despite the advances in knowledge from the social sciences; the listing gives one an unmistakable sense of *déja entendu*. "Research is another troublesome area in which there is considerable ambivalence," with the present trend toward preparing students as consumers of research and not as producers. Well-qualified faculty "is also a very scarce resource" (p. 82).

As for the disregard of the criminal justice system, which has been cited as a prime example of social work neglect, a 1972 survey of students who entered or returned to the field of criminal justice shows an overall percentage decrease as compared to 1967. "This suggests that schools of social work continued to give a relatively low priority to admitting students with criminal justice backgrounds, and to develop curricula and establish work choices in this field" (Senna, 1974, p. 95).

Nevertheless, Kendall (1974/1977) concludes:

> A journey through the *World Guide* gives one a sense of the vitality of the profession throughout the world. There is a clear determination on the part of schools of social work in all regions to be themselves and to drive their roots deep into their own cultural soil. But there is also a historical continuity that goes back to the beginning of social work education, when the first schools put together programs that encompassed knowledge of man and society, humanistic values, and skills in defining and working on social and human problems. Amid the change that envelops us, we can still find enough in common to stand as an international discipline. (p. 83)

On this final note, Kendall sets the *World Guide* firmly into social work's long history of hopeful declamations—though the story social workers tell of themselves is only partially factual, and continuously contradictory. Just a year earlier, Kendall wrote, in "Dream or Nightmare? The Future of Social Work" (1973): "Social work education is in trouble in its essence and in its boundaries. Because the trouble is compounded of controversy and change, it in no way reflects the stillness of death," provided it retains a recognizable core of knowledge and skill and does not degenerate into adventures or activities of much noise and little relation to competence (p. 21).

Certainly, social work is still alive. However, the signs of the 1970s do not enable one to predict with confidence the future well-being of the institution.

Epilogue is still prologue.

DOCUMENTATION

Abbott, Edith, "Field Work and the Training of the Social Worker." In *Proceedings of the National Conference of Charities and Correction, 1915.* Chicago: National Conference of Charities and Correction, 1915.

Abbott, Edith. "The University and Social Welfare." In *Social Welfare and Professional Education.* Chicago: University of Chicago Press, 1931.

Abrams, Philip. *The Origins of British Sociology, 1834–1914.* Chicago: University of Chicago Press, 1968.

Barker, R. G. *Psychology of the Absent Organism.* Unpublished paper, 1961.

Bartlett, Harriett M. "The Generic-Specific Concept in Social Work Education and Practice." In Alfred J. Kahn (Ed.), *Issues in American Social Work.* New York: Columbia University Press, 1959.

Bartlett, Harriett M. "The Place and Use of Knowledge in Social Work Practice." *Social Work,* Vol. IX, no. 3, July 1964, pp. 36–46.

Bartlett, Harriett M. "Social Work Fields of Practice." In *Encyclopedia of Social Work* (Vol. II). New York: National Association of Social Workers, 1971.

Beck, Bertram M. "Shaping America's Social Welfare Policy." In Alfred J. Kahn (Ed.), *Issues in American Social Work.* New York: Columbia University Press, 1959.

Beck, Bertram M. "Social Work Practice." *Proceedings of the National Conference on Social Welfare.* New York: Columbia University Press, 1965.

Berelson, Bernard, and Gary A. Steiner. *Human Behavior: An Inventory of Scientific Findings.* New York: Harcourt, Brace & World, Inc., 1964.

Berger, Peter L. *Invitation to Sociology: A Humanistic Perspective.* New York: Anchor Books, Doubleday & Company, Inc., 1963.

Berne, Eric. *Games People Play: The Psychology of Human Relationships.* New York: Grove Press, Inc., 1964.

Biestek, Felix P. *The Principle of Client Self-Determination in Social Casework.* Washington, D.C.: The Catholic University of America Press, 1951.

Biestek, Felix P. *The Casework Relationship.* Chicago: Loyola University Press, 1957.

Bisno, Herbert. "How Social Will Social Work Be?" *Social Work,* Vol. I, no. 2, April 1956, pp. 12–18.

Blackey, Eileen. "Selection and Preparation of Faculty for Schools of Social Work." *Journal of Education for Social Work*, Vol. I, no. 1, Spring 1965, pp. 5–12.

Bloksberg, Leonard M., and Louis Lowy. "Toward Integrative Learning and Teaching in Social Work: An Analytic Framework." *Journal of Education for Social Work*, Vol. XIII, no. 2, Spring 1977, pp. 3–10.

Boehm, Werner W. *Objectives of the Social Work Curriculum of the Future* (Vol. I of the Curriculum Study). New York: Council on Social Work Education, 1959.

Booth, Charles. "Condition and Occupations of the People of East London and Hackney, 1887." *Journal of the Royal Statistical Society*, 51, June 1888, pp. 276–331.

Booth, Charles. *Life and Labour of the People in London* (3rd ed.) (17 vols.). London: Macmillan & Co., 1902–1903.

Bordua, David J. "Delinquent Subcultures: Sociological Interpretations of Gang Delinquency." *Annals of the American Academy of Political and Social Science*, no. 338, November 1961, pp. 120–136.

Bossard, H. S., and Eleanor Stoker Boll. *The Sociology of Child Development* (3rd ed). New York: Harper & Brothers, 1960.

Bruno, Frank J. (with chapters by Louis Towley). *Trends in Social Work, 1874–1956*. New York: Columbia University Press, 1957.

Burbank, Luther. *The Training of the Human Plant*. New York: Century, 1907.

Burns, Eveline M. "Social Policy: The Stepchild of the Curriculum." In *Education for Social Work*. New York: Council on Social Work Education, 1961.

Burns, Eveline M. "Tomorrow's Social Needs and Social Work Education." *Journal of Education for Social Work*, Vol. II, no. 1, Spring 1966, pp. 10–20.

Burns, Mary E. "Paths to Knowledge: Some Prospects and Problems." *Journal of Education for Social Work*, Vol. I, no. 1, Spring 1965, pp. 13–17.

Carr-Saunders, A. M., and P. A. Wilson. *The Professions*. Oxford: Clarendon Press, 1933.

Cloward, Richard A., and Lloyd E. Ohlin. *Delinquency and Opportunity: A Theory of Delinquent Gangs*. Glencoe, Ill.: The Free Press, 1960.

Cohen, Albert K. *Delinquent Boys: The Culture of the Gang*. Glencoe, Ill.: The Free Press, 1955.

Cohen, Nathan. *Social Work in the American Tradition*. New York: Dryden Press, 1958.

Cormican, Elin J., and John D. Cormican. "The Necessity of Linguistic Sophistication for Social Workers." *Journal of Education for Social Work*, Vol. XIII, no. 2, Spring 1977, pp. 18–21.

Council for Training in Social Work. *Human Growth and Behaviour—As a Subject of Study for Social Workers*. London: Clifton House, 1967.

Council on Social Work Education. *Official Statement of Curriculum Policy for the Master's Degree Program in Graduate Professional Schools of Social Work*. New York: Council on Social Work Education, 1962.

Council on Social Work Education. *Journal of Education for Social Work*, Vol. I, no. 1, Spring 1965.

Council on Social Work Education, *Journal of Education for Social Work*, Vol. I, no. 2, Fall 1965; Vol. II, no. 1, Spring 1966.

Council on Social Work Education. *Curriculum Policy Statement* (November 1969). In *Social Work Education Reporter*, December 1969, insert.

Coyle, Grace L. *Social Science in the Professional Education of Social Workers*. New York: Council on Social Work Education, 1958.

Cramer, Margeryfay. "Fieldwork Preparation for Entrance into Mental Retardation Practice." *Journal of Education for Social Work*, Vol. XIII, no. 1, Winter 1977, pp. 37–43.

Cryns, Arthur G. "Social Work Education and Student Ideology: A Multivariate Study of Professional Education." *Journal of Education for Social Work*, Vol. XIII, no. 1, Winter 1977, pp. 44–51.

Dana, Bess. "Enriching Social Work Education with Mental Retardation Content." *Journal of Education for Social Work*, Vol. I, no. 2, Fall 1965, pp. 5–10.

Dressler, David. *Practice and Theory of Probation and Parole*. New York: Columbia University Press, 1965.

Duehn, Wayne D., and Nazneed Sada Mayadas. "Entrance and Exit Requirements of Professional Social Work Education." *Journal of Education for Social Work*, Vol. XIII, no. 2, Spring 1977, pp. 22–29.

Eaton, Joseph W. "Whence and Whither Social Work? A Sociological Analysis." *Social Work*, Vol. I, no. 1, January 1956, pp. 11–26.

Erikson, Erik H. "Ego Identity and the Psychosocial Moratorium." In Helen L. Witmer and Ruth Kotinsky (Eds.), *New Perspectives for Research on Juvenile Delinquency*. Washington, D.C.: U.S. Department of Health, Education, and Welfare, Children's Bureau, 1955.

Eysenck, Hans J. *The Effects of Psychotherapy*. New York: International Science Press, 1966.

Faatz, Anita J. *The Nature of Choice in Casework Process*. Chapel Hill: University of North Carolina Press, 1953.

Faris, Robert E. L. *Chicago Sociology, 1920–1932*. Chicago: University of Chicago Press, 1967.

Finestone, Samuel. "A Memorandum on Research into Social Work Education." *Journal of Education for Social Work*, Vol. I, no. 1, Spring 1965, pp. 18–25.

Fink, Arthur E., Everett E. Wilson, and Merrill B. Conover. *The Field of Social Work* (4th ed.). New York: Holt, Rinehart and Winston, Inc., 1963.

Flexner, Abraham. "Is Social Work a Profession?" *Proceedings of the National Conference of Charities and Correction, 1915*. Chicago: National Conference of Charities and Correction, 1915.

Form, William H. "Social Power and Social Welfare." In Robert Morris (Ed.), *Centrally Planned Change: Prospects and Concepts*. New York: National Association of Social Workers, 1964.

Fraiberg, Selma H. *The Magic Years: Understanding and Handling the Problems of Early Childhood*. New York: Charles Scribner's Sons, 1959.

Gardner, John W. "Remarks by John W. Gardner." *Journal of Education for Social Work*, Vol. II, no. 1, Spring 1966, pp. 5–9.

Geis, Gilbert. "Liberal Education and Social Welfare: Educational Choices and Their Consequences." *Journal of Education for Social Work*, Vol. I, no. 1, Spring 1965, pp. 26–32.

Glasgow, Douglas. "The Black Thrust for Vitality: The Impact on Social Work Education." *Journal of Education for Social Work*, Vol. VII, no. 2, Spring 1971, pp. 9–18.

Glasser, William. *Reality Therapy: A New Approach to Psychiatry*. New York: Harper & Row, Publishers, Inc., 1965.

Glover, E. Elizabeth, and Joseph H. Reid. "Unmet and Future Needs." *Annals of the American Academy of Political and Social Science*, no. 355, September 1964, pp. 9–19.

Gordon, William E. "Toward a Social Work Frame of Reference." *Journal of Education for Social Work*, Vol. I, no. 2, Fall 1965, pp. 19–26.

Gouldner, Alvin W., and S. N. Miller (Eds.). *Applied Sociology: Opportunities and Problems*. New York: The Free Press, 1965.

Greene, Maxine. "The Humanities and Social Work Education." *Journal of Education for Social Work*, Vol. II, no. 1, Spring 1966, pp. 21–31.

Greenwood, Ernest. "Social Science and Social Work: A Theory of Their Relationship." *Social Service Review*, Vol. XXIX, no. 1, March 1955, pp. 20–33.

Greenwood, Ernest. "Attributes of a Profession." *Social Work*, Vol. II, no. 3, July 1957, pp. 44–55.

Guttmacher, Manfred S. "The Psychiatric Approach to Crime and Corrections." *Law and Contemporary Problems*, Vol. XXIII, Autumn 1958, pp. 633–649.

Hakeem, Michael. "A Critique of the Psychiatric Approach to the Prevention of Juvenile Delinquency." In Rose Giallombardo (Ed.), *Juvenile Delinquency: A Book of Readings* (2nd ed.). New York: John Wiley and Sons, Inc., 1972.

Hale, Mark P. "The Parameters of Agency-School Social Work Educational Planning." *Journal of Education for Social Work*, Vol. II, no. 1, Spring 1966, pp. 32–40.

Halleck, Seymour L. "The Impact of Professional Dishonesty on Behavior of Disturbed Adolescents." In Arthur B. Shostak (Ed.), *Sociology in Action: Case Studies in Social Problems and Directed Social Change*. Homewood, Ill.: The Dorsey Press, 1966.

Halmos, Paul. *The Faith of the Counsellors: A Study in the Theory and Practice of Social Case Work and Psychotherapy*. New York: Schocken Books, 1966.

Hamilton, Gordon. *Theory and Practice of Social Case Work* (2nd ed.). New York: The New York School of Social Work, Columbia University, 1951.

Harrington, Michael. *The Other America: Poverty in the United States.* New York: The Macmillan Company, 1962.

Harris, Thomas A. *I'm OK—You're OK: A Practical Guide to Transactional Analysis.* New York: Harper & Row, Publishers, Inc., 1967.

Hartman, Charles Yecheskel. *Social Casework and Pastoral Counseling: A Study of Perceived Similarities and Differences in the Goals and Methods of Two Helping Professions.* Abstract, doctoral dissertation, Washington University, St. Louis, Missouri, 1962.

Heffernan, W. Joseph, Jr. "Political Activity and Social Work Executives." *Social Work,* Vol. IX, no. 2, April 1964, pp. 18–23.

Hockenstad, Merl C., Jr. "Higher Education and the Human Service Professions: What Role for Social Work?" *Journal of Education for Social Work,* Vol. XIII, no. 2, Spring 1977, pp. 52–59.

Hollis, Ernest W., and Alice L. Taylor. *Social Work Education in the United States.* New York: Columbia University Press, 1951.

Hollis, Florence. *Casework: A Psychosocial Therapy.* New York: Random House, Inc., 1964.

Horowitz, Gideon. "New Curriculum Policy Statement: Freedom and/or Regulation—1." *Journal of Education for Social Work,* Vol. VII, no. 2, Spring 1971, pp. 41–46.

Hunter, David R. "Slums and Social Work, or Wishes and the Double Negative." In Bernard Rosenberg, Israel Gerver, and F. William Howton (Eds.), *Mass Society in Crisis: Case Studies in Social Problems and Social Pathology.* New York: The Macmillan Company, 1964.

Hunter, Mary "Ski," and Dennis Soleeby. "Spirit and Substance: Beginnings in the Education of Radical Social Workers." *Journal of Education for Social Work,* Vol. XIII, no. 2, Spring 1977, pp. 60–67.

International Association of Schools of Social Work. *World Guide to Social Work Education.* New York: International Association of Schools of Social Work, 1973.

"Joint Statement on Rights and Freedoms of Students." *AAUP Bulletin,* Vol. LI, no. 4, Winter 1967, p. 365.

Kadushin, Alfred. "Prestige of Social Work—Facts and Factors." *Social Work,* Vol. III, no. 2, April 1958, pp. 37–43.

Kadushin, Alfred. "The Knowledge Base of Social Work." In Alfred J. Kahn (Ed.), *Issues in American Social Work.* New York: Columbia University Press, 1959.

Kadushin, Alfred. "Two Problems of the Graduate Program: Level and Content." *Journal of Education for Social Work,* Vol. I, no. 1, Spring 1965, pp. 33–46.

Kahn, Alfred J. (Ed.). *Issues in American Social Work.* New York: Columbia University Press, 1959.

Katz, Arthur J. "New Curriculum Policy Statement: Freedom and/or Regulation—2." *Journal of Education for Social Work*, Vol. VII, no. 2, Spring 1971, pp. 47–54.

Karpf, Maurice J. *The Scientific Basis of Social Work*. New York: Columbia University Press, 1931.

Keith-Lucas, Alan. "A Critique of the Principle of Client Self-Determination." *Social Work*, Vol. VIII, no. 3, July 1963, pp. 66–71.

Kelling, George. "Caught in a Crossfire of Concepts—Correction and the Dilemmas of Social Work." *Crime and Delinquency*, Vol. XIV, no. 1, January 1968, pp. 26–30.

Kendall, Katherine A. "A Conceptual Framework for the Social Work Curriculum of Tomorrow." *Social Service Review*, Vol. XXVII, no. 1, March 1953, pp. 15–26.

Kendall, Katherine A. "Dream or Nightmare? The Future of Social Work." *Journal of Education for Social Work*, Vol. IX, no. 2, Spring 1973, pp. 13-23.

Kendall, Katherine A. "Cross-National Review of Social Work Education" (Address to the Seventeenth International Congress of Schools of Social Work, Nairobi, Kenya, July 1974). *Journal of Education for Social Work*, Vol. XIII, no. 2, Spring 1977, pp. 76–83.

Kindelsperger, Walter L. "Responsible Entry into the Profession—Some Current Issues." *Journal of Education for Social Work*, Vol. II, no. 1, Spring 1966, pp. 41–51.

Klein, Philip. *From Philanthropy to Social Welfare: An American Cultural Perspective*. San Francisco: Jossey-Bass, Inc., 1968.

Lauffer, Armand. "A New Breed of Social Actionist Comes to Social Work: The Community Organization Student." *Journal of Education for Social Work*, Vol. VII, no. 1, Winter 1971, pp. 43–54.

Levenstein, Sidney. *Private Practice in Social Casework: A Profession's Changing Pattern*. New York: Columbia University Press, 1964.

Lowy, Louis, "Social Work and Social Statesmanship." *Social Work*, Vol. V, no. 2, April 1960, pp. 97–104.

Lowy, Louis, Leonard M. Bloksberg, and Herbert J. Walberg. *Integrative Learning and Teaching in Schools of Social Work*. New York: Association Press, 1971.

Lurie, Harry L. "The Responsibilities of a Socially Oriented Profession." In Cora Kasius (Ed.), *Principles and Techniques in Social Casework*. New York: Harper, 1954.

MacDonald, Mary E. "Social Work Research: A Perspective." In Norman A. Polansky (Ed.), *Social Work Research*. Chicago: University of Chicago Press, 1960.

Mannheim, Karl. *Man and Society in an Age of Reconstruction*. London: Kegan Paul, Trench, Trubner and Company, 1946.

Marcus, Grace F. "The Generic and Specific in Social Case Work—Recent Developments in Our Thinking." *News-Letter*, American Association of Psychiatric Social Workers, Vol. VII, 1938–39, pp. 3–4.

Martin, John M., and Joseph P. Fitzpatrick. *Delinquent Behavior: A Redefinition of the Problem.* New York: Random House, Inc., 1964.

Matza, David. "Poverty and Disrepute." In Robert K. Merton and Robert Nisbet (Eds.), *Contemporary Social Problems* (3rd ed.). New York: Harcourt Brace Jovanovich, Inc., 1971.

Mayhew, Henry. *London Labour and the London Poor* (4 vols.). New York: Dover Publications, Inc., 1968. (Originally published in 1861–1862)

McBroom, Elizabeth. "Individual, Group, and Community in the Behavior Sequence." *Journal of Education for Social Work*, Vol. I, no. 2, Fall 1965, pp. 27–34.

Mencher, Samuel. "The Future for Voluntaryism in American Social Welfare." In Alfred J. Kahn (Ed.), *Issues in American Social Work.* New York: Columbia University Press, 1959.

Merton, Robert K. "Social Structure and Anomie." *American Sociological Review*, Vol. III, October 1938, pp. 672–682.

Merton, Robert K., and Robert A. Nisbet (Eds.). *Contemporary Social Problems* (3rd ed.). New York: Harcourt, Brace & World, Inc., 1971.

Meyer, Henry J. "Professionalism and Social Work." In Alfred J. Kahn (Ed.), *Issues in American Social Work.* New York: Columbia University Press, 1959.

Mills, C. Wright. "The Professional Ideology of Social Pathologists." *American Journal of Sociology*, Vol. XLIX, no. 2, September 1943, pp. 165–180.

Moody, Joseph N. "Leo XIII and the Social Crisis." In Edward T. Gargan (Ed.), *Leo XIII and the Modern World.* New York: Sheed and Ward, 1961.

Morris, Cherry (Ed.). *Social Case-Work in Great Britain* (2nd ed.). London: Faber, 1955.

Mossman, Mereb S. "Review: Gordon J. Aldridge and Earl J. McGrath, *Liberal Education and Social Work.*" *Journal of Education for Social Work*, Vol. I, no. 2, Fall 1965, pp. 61–65.

National Association of Social Workers. *Goals of Public Social Policy.* New York: National Association of Social Workers, 1963.

National Association of Social Workers. *Midnight Raids.* New York: National Association of Social Workers, 1964.

Nisbet, Robert A. "The Study of Social Problems." In Robert K. Merton and Robert A. Nisbet (Eds.), *Contemporary Social Problems* (2nd ed.). New York: Harcourt, Brace & World, Inc., 1966.

Oswald, Ida M. "Through the Looking Glass: Adventure in Television." *Journal of Education for Social Work*, Vol. I, no. 1, Spring 1965, pp. 47–55.

Peirce, Frank J. "Student Involvement: Participatory Democracy or Adult Socialization?" *Journal of Education for Social Work*, Vol. VI, no. 2, Fall 1970, pp. 21–26.

Perlman, Helen Harris. "Social Casework." In Russell H. Kurtz (Ed.), *Social Work Yearbook 1960.* New York: National Association of Social Workers, 1960.

Pfautz, Harold W. (Ed.). *Charles Booth on the City: Physical Pattern and Social Structure.* Chicago: University of Chicago Press, 1967.

Polansky, Norman A. "The Professional Identity in Social Work." In Alfred J. Kahn (Ed.), *Issues in American Social Work.* New York: Columbia University Press, 1959.

"Poor Law." *Encyclopaedia Britannica* (Vol. 18). Chicago: William Benton, Publisher, 1966.

President's Commission on Law Enforcement and Administration of Justice. *The Challenge of Crime in a Free Society.* Washington, D.C.: U.S. Government Printing Office, 1967.

President's Commission on Law Enforcement and Administration of Justice, Task Force on Juvenile Delinquency. *Juvenile Delinquency and Youth Crime.* Washington, D.C.: U.S. Government Printing Office, 1967.

Pumphrey, Muriel W. *The Teaching of Values and Ethics in Social Work Education* (Vol. XIII of the Curriculum Study). New York: Council on Social Work Education, 1959.

Pumphrey, Muriel W. "Mary E. Richmond—The Practitioner." *Social Casework*, Vol. XLII, no. 8, October 1961, pp. 375–385.

Pumphrey, Ralph E., and Muriel W. Pumphrey (Eds.). *The Heritage of American Social Work: Readings in Its Philosophical and Institutional Development.* New York: Columbia University Press, 1961.

Reich, Charles A. "Midnight Welfare Searches and the Social Security Act." *Yale Law Journal*, Vol. LXXII, no. 7, June 1963, pp. 1347–1360.

Reich, Charles A. "The New Property." *Yale Law Journal*, Vol. LXXIII, no. 5, April 1964, pp. 733–787.

Ribicoff, Abraham. "Politics and Social Workers." *Social Work*, Vol. VII, no. 2, April 1962, pp. 3–6.

Rich, Margaret E. "Current Trends in Social Adjustment Through Individualized Treatment." In *Report of the Third International Conference on Social Work: London, 1936.* London: Le Play House, 1938.

Richan, Willard C. "New Curriculum Policy Statement: The Problem of Professional Cohesion—3." *Journal of Education for Social Work*, Vol. VII, no. 2, Spring 1971, pp. 55–60.

Richan, Willard C., and Allan R. Mendelsohn. *Social Work: The Unloved Profession.* New York: New Viewpoints, Franklin Watts, Inc., 1973.

Richmond Mary E. *Social Diagnosis.* New York: Russell Sage Foundation, 1917.

Richmond, Mary E. "The Retail Method of Reform." In *The Long View.* New York: Russell Sage Foundation, 1930.

Sanders, Marion K. "Social Work: A Profession Chasing Its Tail." *Harper's Magazine*, March 1957, pp. 56–62.

Schofield, William. *Psychotherapy: The Purchase of Friendship.* Englewood Cliffs, N.J.: Prentice-Hall, Inc., 1964.

Schottland, Charles L. "Review: *Task Force Report on Social Work Education and Manpower.*" *Journal of Education for Social Work*, Vol. II, no. 1, Spring 1966, pp. 71–75.

Schubert, Margaret S. "Curriculum Policy Dilemmas in Field Instruction." *Journal of Education for Social Work*, Vol. I, no. 2, Fall 1965, pp. 35–46.

Senna, Joseph J. "The Role of the Graduate School of Social Work in Criminal Justice Higher Education." *Journal of Education for Social Work*, Vol. X, no. 2, Spring 1974, pp. 92–98.

Simey, T. S., and M. B. Simey. *Charles Booth, Social Scientist.* London: Oxford University Press, 1960.

Siporin, Max. "Review of Noel Timms' *Casework in the Child Care Service, 1962; Social Casework, 1964; Psychiatric Social Work in Great Britain, 1939–1962, 1964.*" *Journal of Education for Social Work*, Vol. I, no. 1, Spring 1965, pp. 76–82.

Smalley, Ruth Elizabeth. *Theory for Social Work Practice.* New York: Columbia University Press, 1967.

Smith, Elliott Dunlap. "Education and the Task of Making Social Work Professional." *Social Service Review*, Vol. XXXI, no. 1, March 1957, pp. 1–10.

Stein, Herman D. "Cross-Currents in Practice, Undergraduate, and Graduate Education in Social Work." *Journal of Education for Social Work*, Vol. I, no. 1, Spring 1965, pp. 56–67.

Stein, Herman D. "Professions and Universities." *Journal of Education for Social Work*, Vol. IV, no. 2, Fall 1968, pp. 53–66.

Studt, Elliot. *Education for Social Workers in the Correctional Field.* New York: Council on Social Work Education, 1959.

Sutherland, Edwin H. *Principles of Criminology* (5th ed.). New York: J. B. Lippincott Co., 1955.

Szasz, Thomas S. *The Myth of Mental Illness: Foundations of a Theory of Personal Conflict.* New York: Hoerber Medical Division, Harper & Row, Publishers, Inc., 1961.

Tappan, Paul W. *Juvenile Delinquency.* New York: McGraw-Hill, Inc., 1949.

Tarter, Donald E. "Heeding Skinner's Call: Toward the Development of a Social Technology." *The American Sociologist*, Vol. VIII, no. 4, November 1973, pp. 153–158.

Thomas, W. I., and Florian Znaniecki. *The Polish Peasant in Europe and America* (2nd ed.). New York: Alfred A. Knopf, Inc., 1927.

Thrasher, Frederic M. *The Gang,* Chicago: University of Chicago Press, 1927; Rev. Ed., 1939.

Titmuss, Richard M. *Essays on "The Welfare State."* London: Ruskin House, George Allen & Unwin, Ltd., 1958.

Titmuss, Richard M. "The Relationship Between Schools of Social Work, Social Research, and Social Policy" (Address to the Twelfth International Congress of Schools of Social Work, Athens, Greece, September 1964). *Journal of Education for Social Work*, Vol. I, no. 1, Spring 1965, pp. 68–75.

Todd, Arthur James. *The Scientific Spirit and Social Work.* New York: The Macmillan Company, 1919.

Towle, Charlotte. "Social Work: Cause and Function, 1961." *Social Case-work*, Vol. XLII, no. 8, October 1961, pp. 385–397.

United Nations, Department of Economic and Social Affairs. *Training for Social Work: Third International Survey.* New York: United Nations, Department of Economic and Social Affairs, 1958.

Varley, Barbara K. "Socialization in Social Work Executives." *Social Work*, Vol. VIII, no. 3, July 1963, pp. 102–109.

Vigilante, Joseph L. "Review: *Changing Services for Changing Clients* (National Association of Social Workers, 1969)." *Journal of Education for Social Work*, Vol. VI, no. 1, Spring 1970, pp. 81–86.

Vigilante, Joseph L. "Student Participation in Decision-Making in Schools of Social Work." *Journal of Education for Social Work*, Fall 1970, Vol. VI, no. 2, pp. 51–60.

Vinter, Robert D. "Analysis of Treatment Organizations." *Social Work*, Vol. VIII, no. 3, July 1963, pp. 3–15.

Wallace, David. "The Chemung County Evaluation of Casework Service to Dependent Multiproblem Families—Another Problem Outcome." *Social Service Review*, Vol. XLI, no. 4, pp. 379–389.

Walsh, Ethel. "Research and Teaching of Casework." *Journal of Education for Social Work*, Vol. I, no. 2, Fall 1965, pp. 47–52.

Walsh, Mary Elizabeth. *The Saints and Social Work.* Silver Spring, Md.: The Preservation of the Faith, 1937.

Webb, Beatrice. *My Apprenticeship.* New York: Longmans, Green & Co., 1926.

Winnicott, Clare. "Casework and Agency Function." *Case Conference*, Vol. VIII, 1962, pp. 178–184.

Woodroofe, Kathleen. *From Charity to Social Work in England and the United States.* London: Routledge and Kegan Paul, 1962.

Wootton, Barbara (assisted by Vera G. Seal and Rosalind Chambers). *Social Science and Social Pathology.* London: Ruskin House, George Allen & Unwin, Ltd., 1959.

Wootton, Barbara. *In a World I Never Made: Autobiographical Reflections.* Toronto: University of Toronto Press, 1967; London: George Allen & Unwin, Ltd., 1967.

Younghusband, Eileen. *Social Work and Social Change.* London: Ruskin House, George Allen & Unwin, Ltd., 1964.

Younghusband, Eileen. "Intercultural Aspects of Social Work." *Journal of Education for Social Work*, Vol. II, no. 1, Spring 1966, pp. 59–65.

Younghusband, Eileen. "The Teacher in Education for Social Work." *Social Service Review*, Vol. XLI, no. 4, December 1967, pp. 359–370.

ABOUT THE AUTHOR

Dr. Marie A. Mathews is a sociologist with a background in social work, notably with the Family Court of Chicago and the Wisconsin School for Girls. An educational consultant to the St. Louis-St. Louis County White House Conference on the Education of the Disadvantaged Youth in 1962 and editor of the Conference Working Papers, Dr. Mathews also was a lecturer in Juvenile Delinquency at the Seminary Institute funded by the President's Committee on Juvenile Delinquency during the summers of 1965 and 1966.

In the 70's she was a founding member of the Family Relations Center, Louisville, and served as President of the Board of Directors. She also played an initiating role in the reorganization of Dismas House, a half-way house for ex-offenders.

Dr. Mathews obtained her A.B. at Mundelein College, Chicago; her M.S.A. at Loyola University, Chicago; and her Ph.D. in Sociology at St. Louis University. She has taught at Maryville College, St. Louis; in St. Louis University's Department of Sociology and its School of Social Service. Dr. Mathews is presently Professor of Sociology at Bellarmine College, Louisville, and chaired the Department of Sociology from 1971-1979.

Dr. Mathews and her husband, Dr. Paul L. Mathews, make their home in Louisville, Kentucky.